War and Peas

Funny Comics for Dirty Lovers

Jonathan Kunz and Elizabeth Pich

Andrews McMeel
PUBLISHING®

A GOOD BOOK

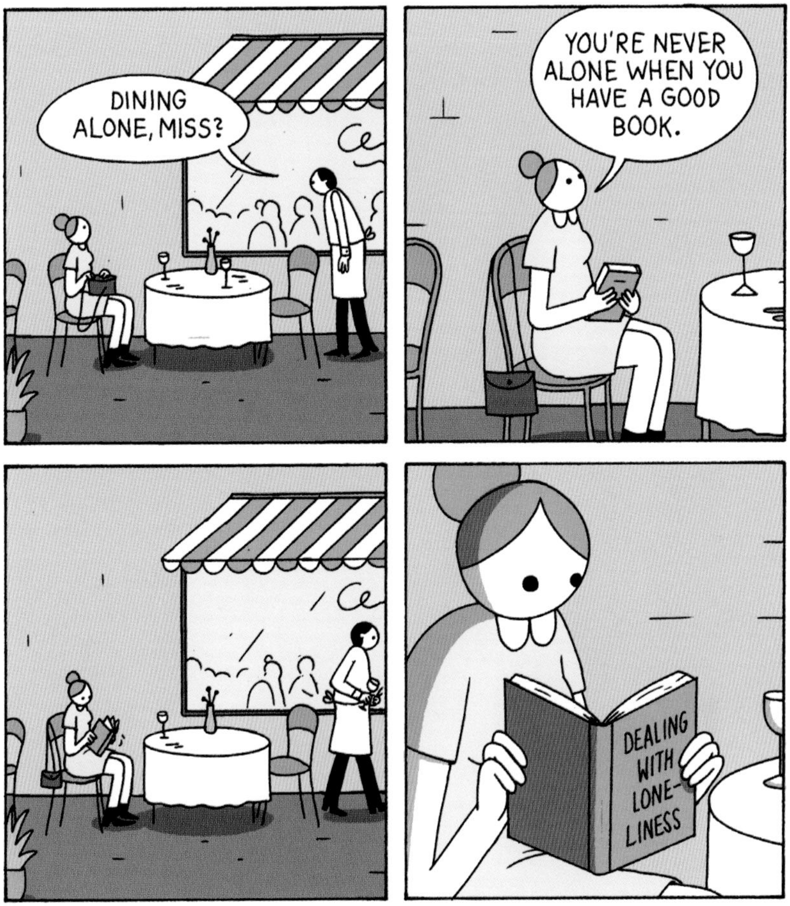
DINING ALONE, MISS?
YOU'RE NEVER ALONE WHEN YOU HAVE A GOOD BOOK.
DEALING WITH LONE-LINESS

DISTRACTION

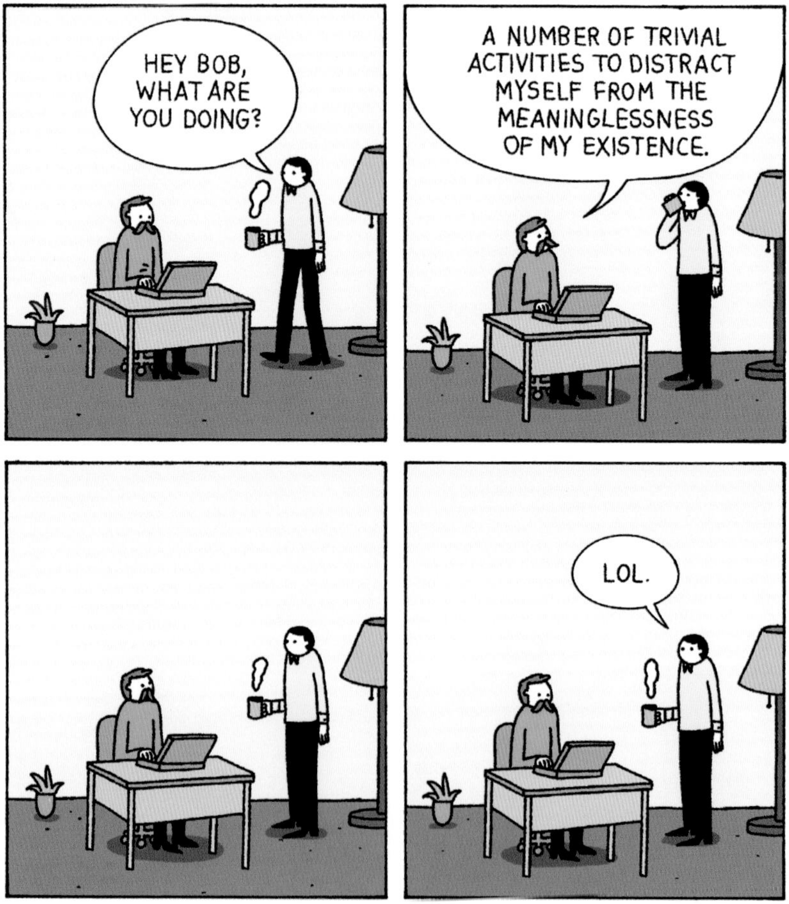
HEY BOB, WHAT ARE YOU DOING?
A NUMBER OF TRIVIAL ACTIVITIES TO DISTRACT MYSELF FROM THE MEANINGLESSNESS OF MY EXISTENCE.
LOL.

I LOVE MY JOB

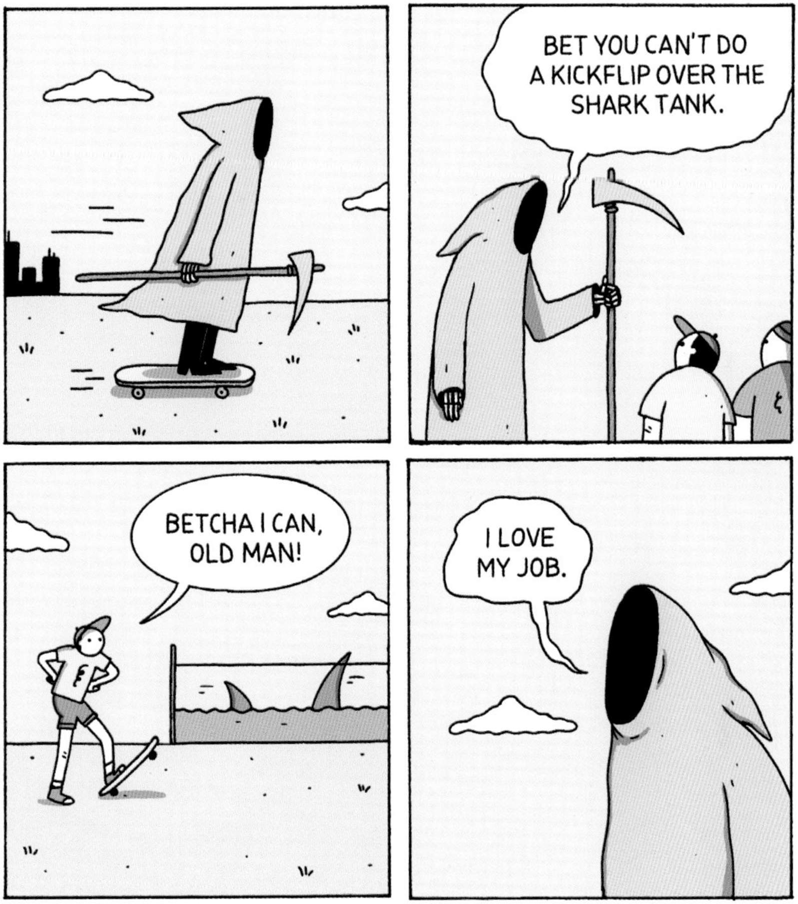
BET YOU CAN'T DO A KICKFLIP OVER THE SHARK TANK.
BETCHA I CAN, OLD MAN!
I LOVE MY JOB.

WOMEN IN SCIENCE

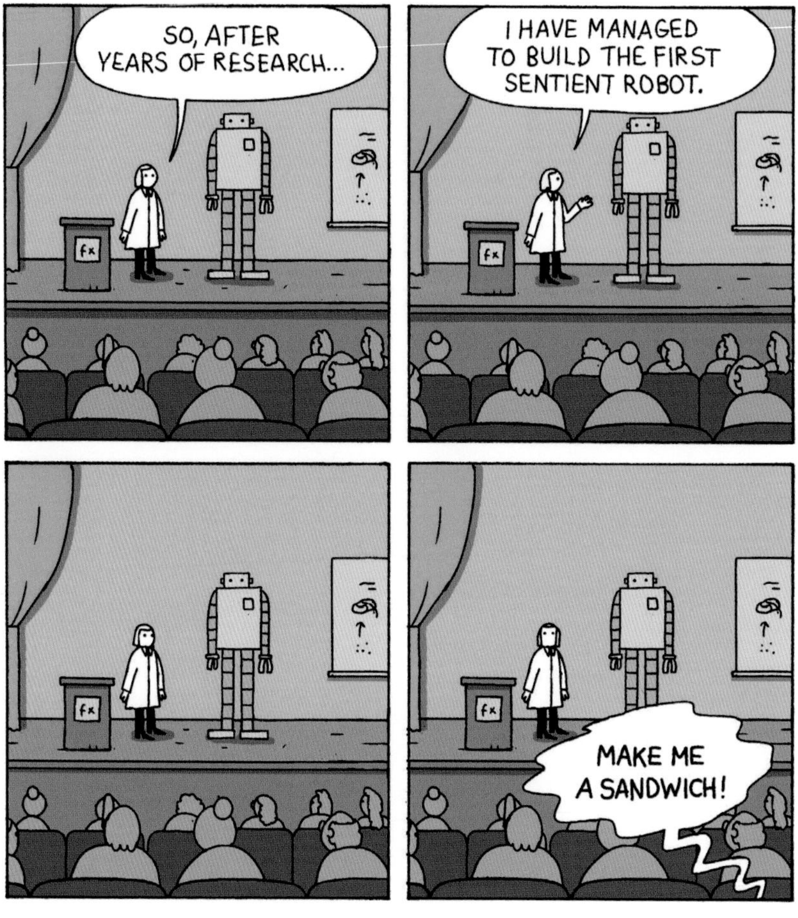
SO, AFTER YEARS OF RESEARCH...
I HAVE MANAGED TO BUILD THE FIRST SENTIENT ROBOT.
MAKE ME A SANDWICH!

PIZZA SURPRISE

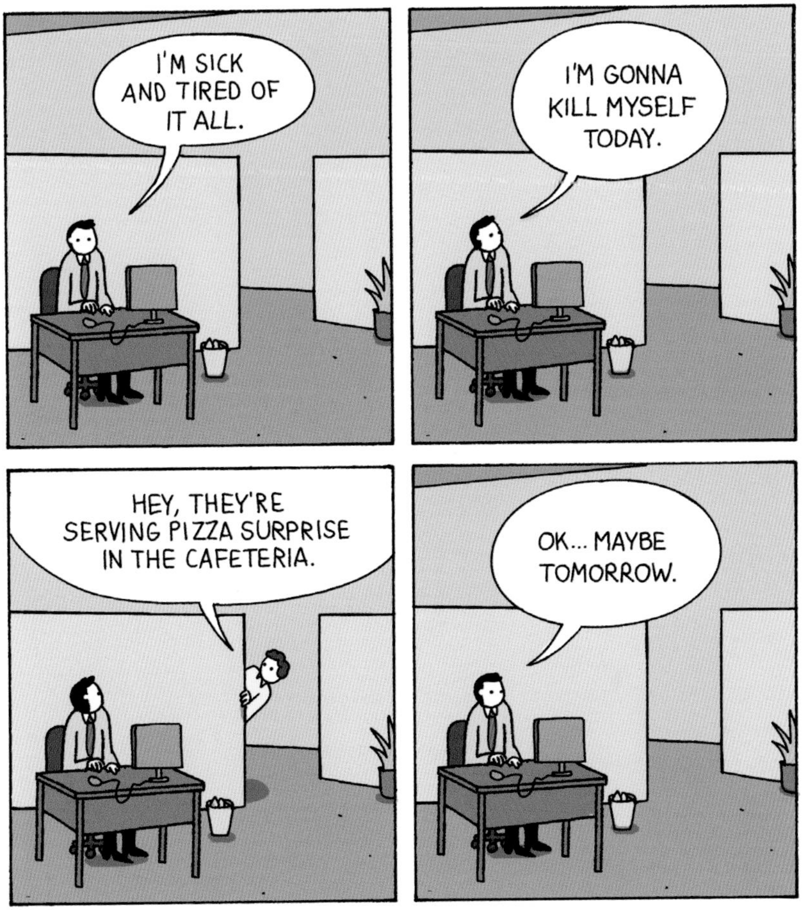
I'M SICK AND TIRED OF IT ALL.
I'M GONNA KILL MYSELF TODAY.
HEY, THEY'RE SERVING PIZZA SURPRISE IN THE CAFETERIA.
OK... MAYBE TOMORROW.

REFUND

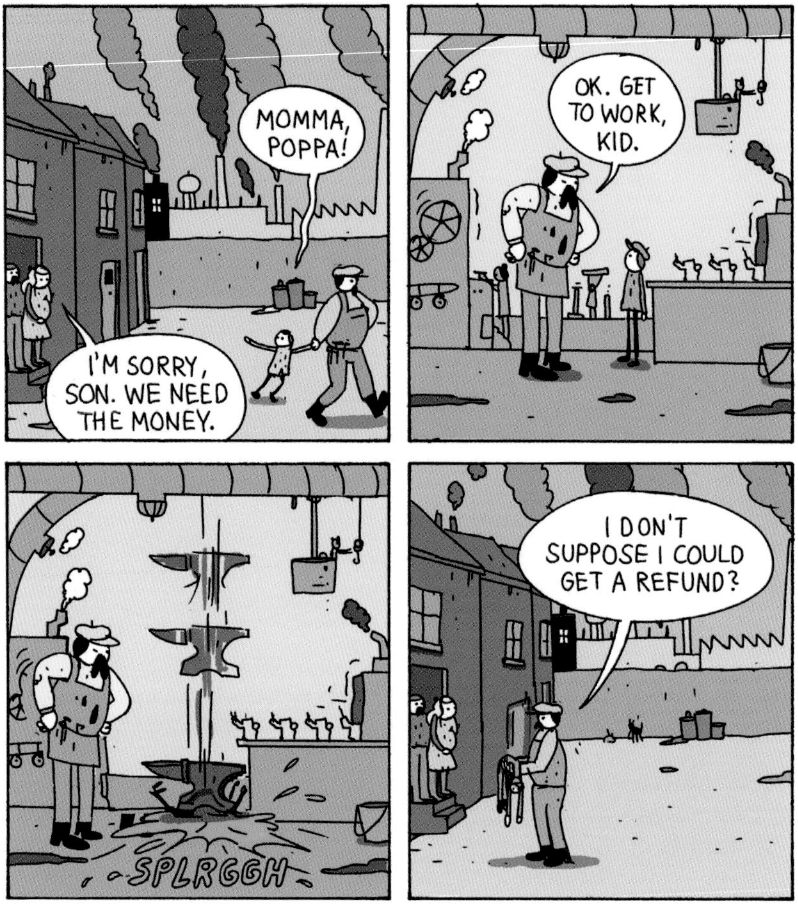

MOMMA, POPPA!
I'M SORRY, SON. WE NEED THE MONEY.
OK. GET TO WORK, KID.
SPLRGGH
I DON'T SUPPOSE I COULD GET A REFUND?

STAY COOL

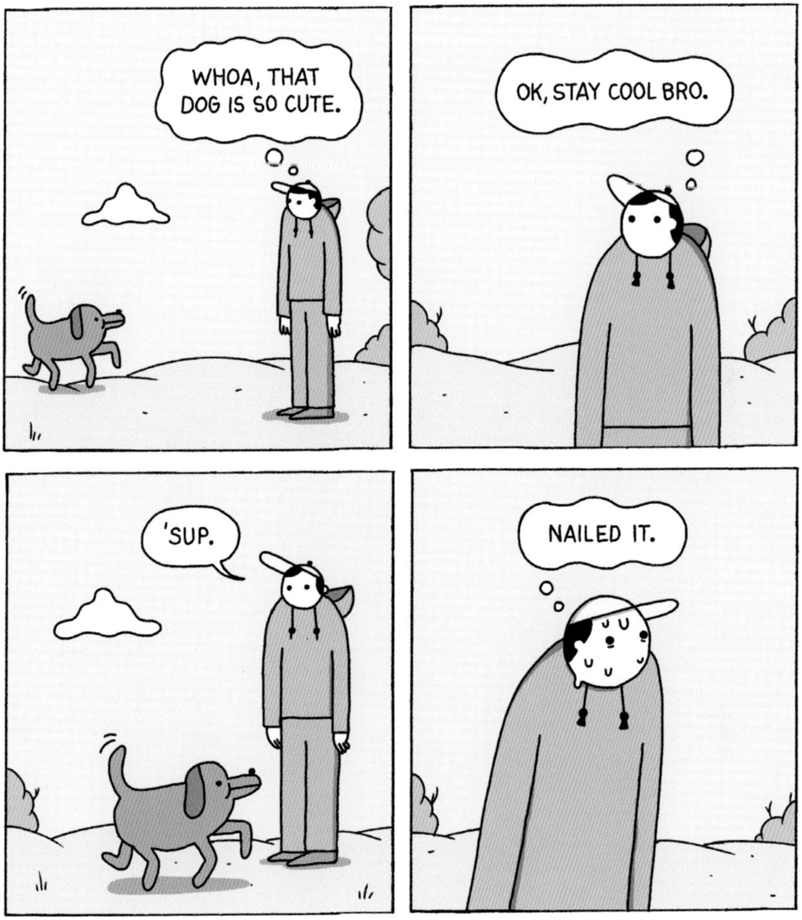

WHOA, THAT DOG IS SO CUTE.
OK, STAY COOL BRO.
'SUP.
NAILED IT.

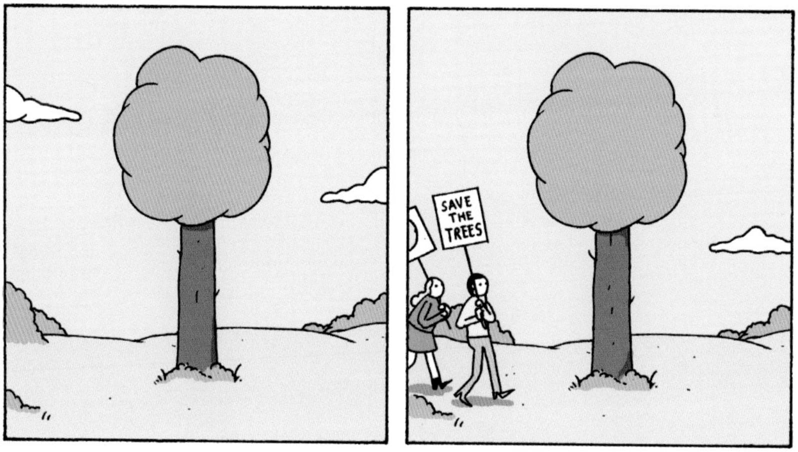
SAVE THE TREES

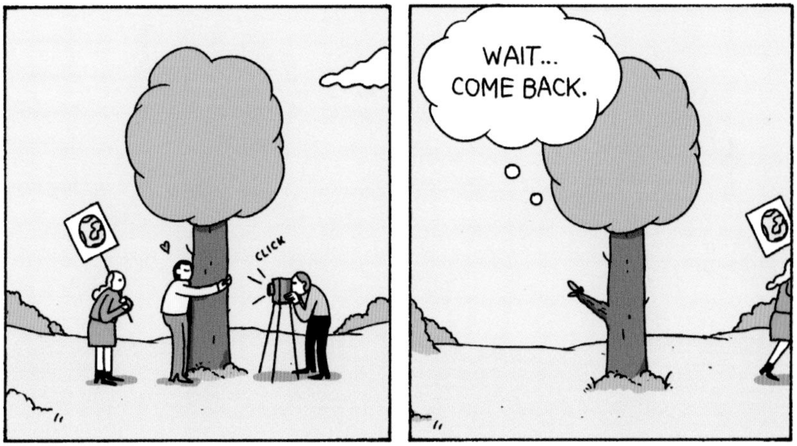
CLICK
WAIT...
COME BACK.

EX-HUSBAND

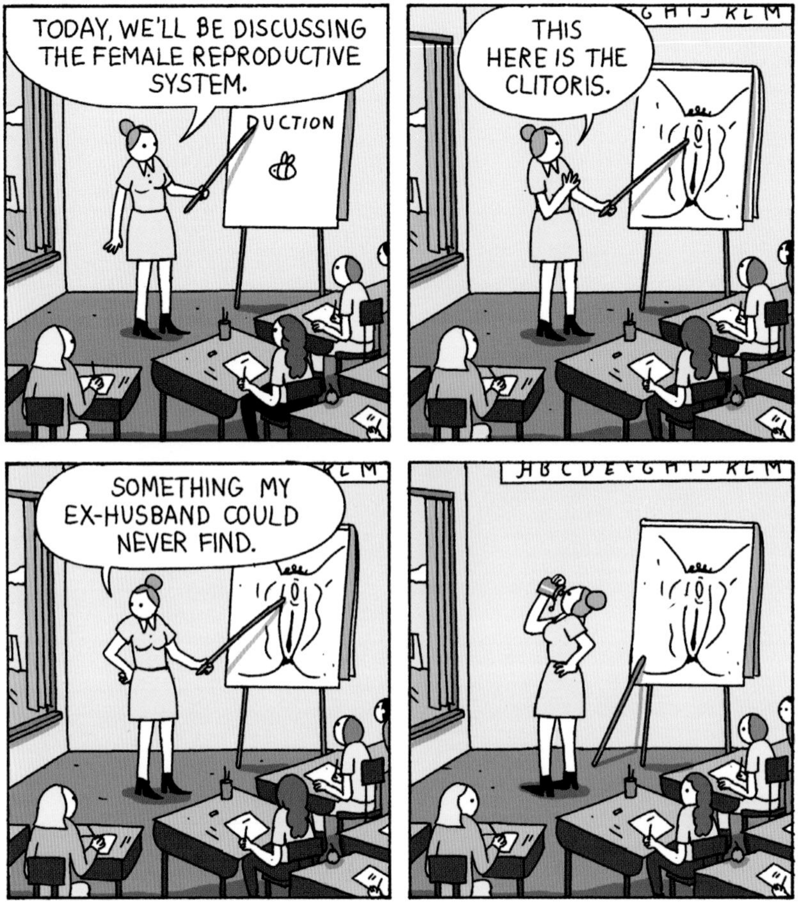
TODAY, WE'LL BE DISCUSSING THE FEMALE REPRODUCTIVE SYSTEM.
DUCTION
THIS HERE IS THE CLITORIS.
SOMETHING MY EX-HUSBAND COULD NEVER FIND.

GOOD FRIEND

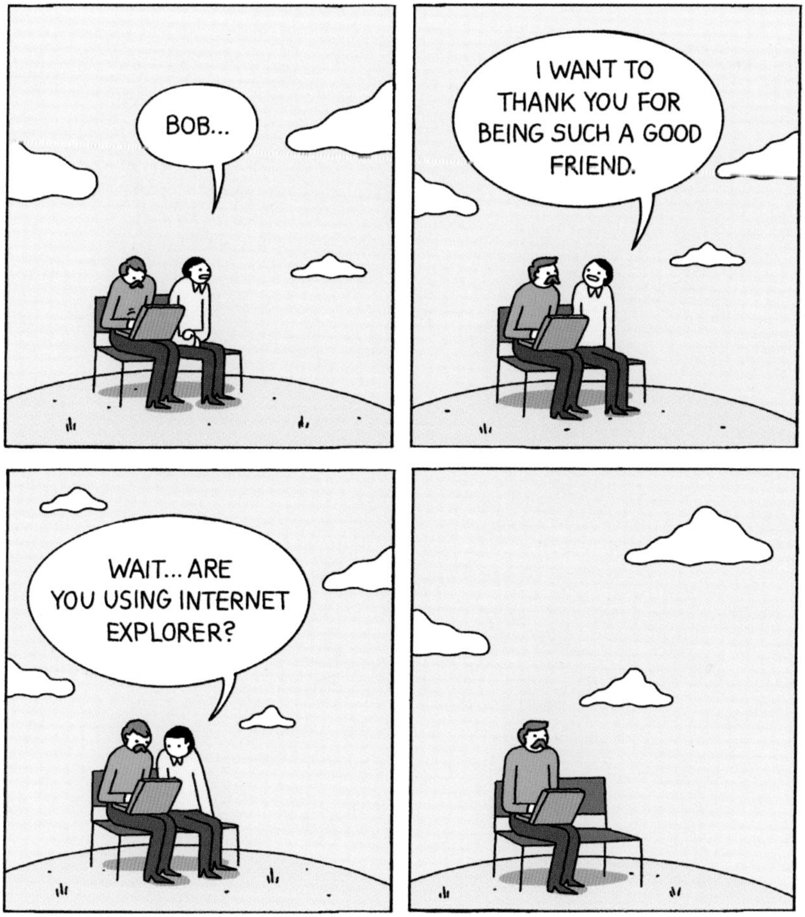
BOB...
I WANT TO THANK YOU FOR BEING SUCH A GOOD FRIEND.
WAIT... ARE YOU USING INTERNET EXPLORER?

BE READY

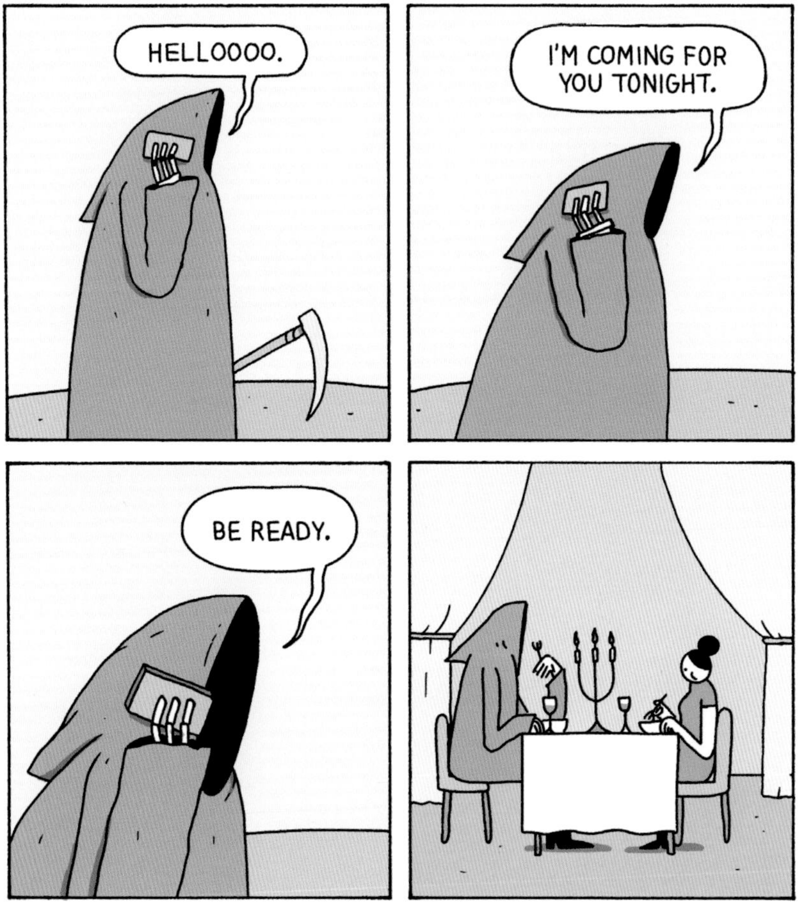
HELLOOOO.
I'M COMING FOR YOU TONIGHT.
BE READY.

EMO MODULE

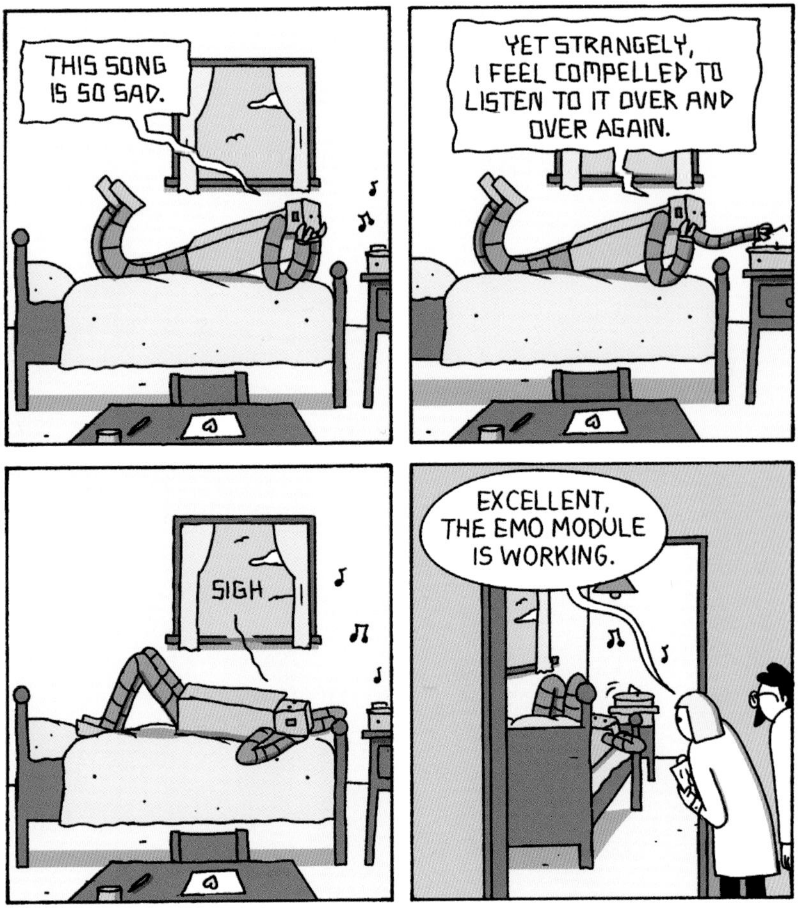
THIS SONG IS SO SAD.
YET STRANGELY, I FEEL COMPELLED TO LISTEN TO IT OVER AND OVER AGAIN.
SIGH
EXCELLENT, THE EMO MODULE IS WORKING.

LUCKY PENNY

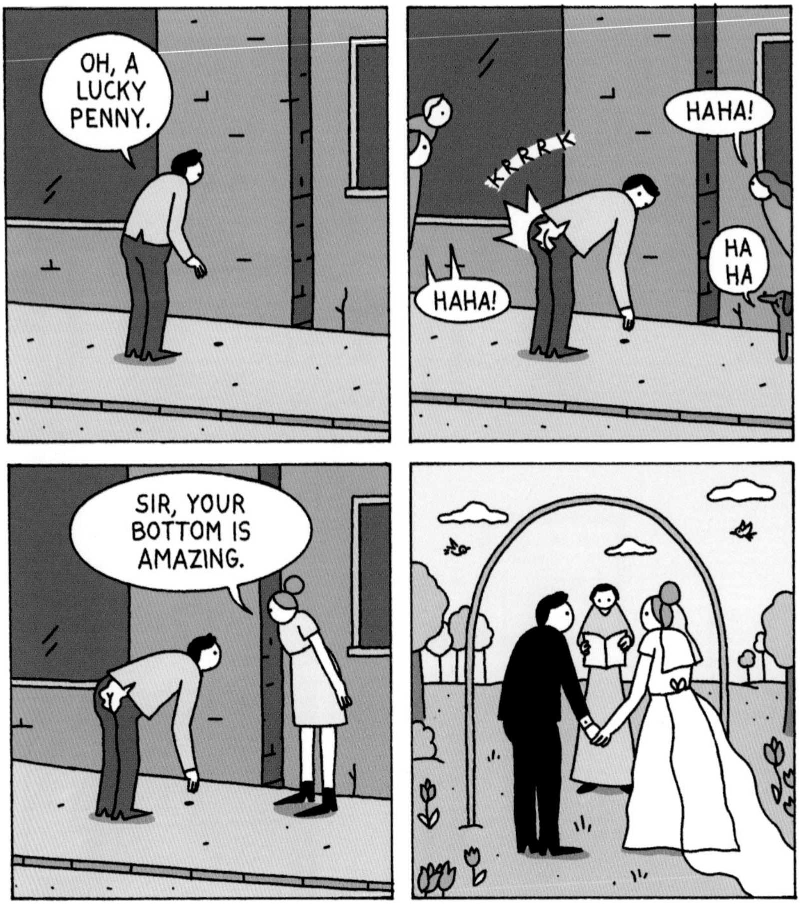

OH, A LUCKY PENNY.
KRRRK
HAHA!
HAHA!
HA HA
SIR, YOUR BOTTOM IS AMAZING.

PUT IT IN THE OVEN

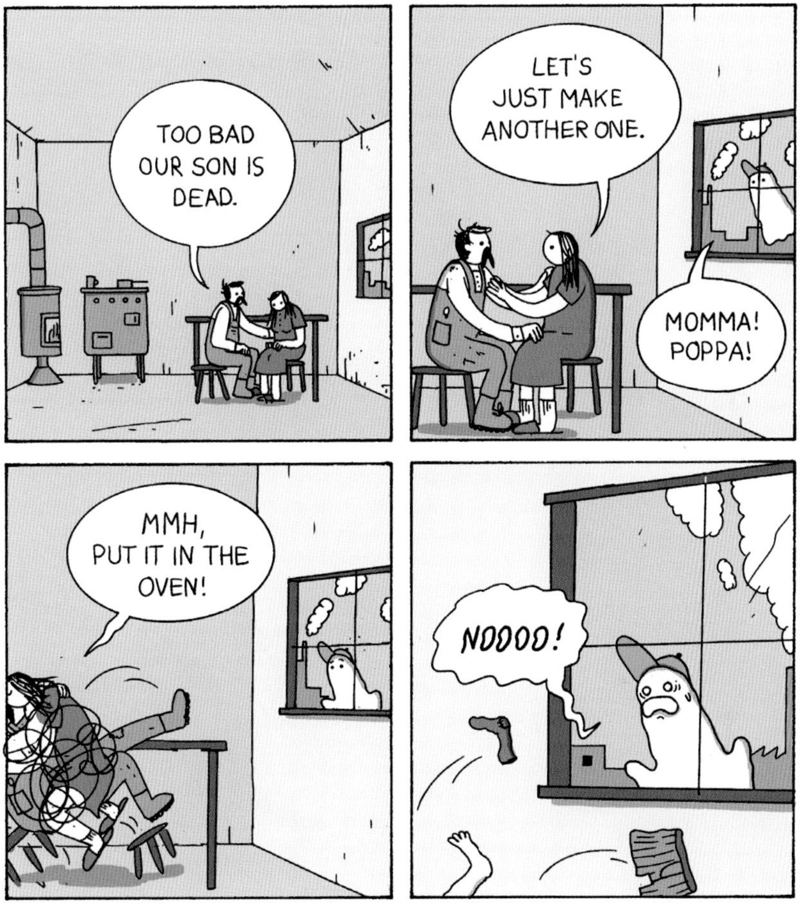
TOO BAD OUR SON IS DEAD.
LET'S JUST MAKE ANOTHER ONE.
MOMMA! POPPA!
MMH, PUT IT IN THE OVEN!
NOOOO!

HIDE AND SEEK

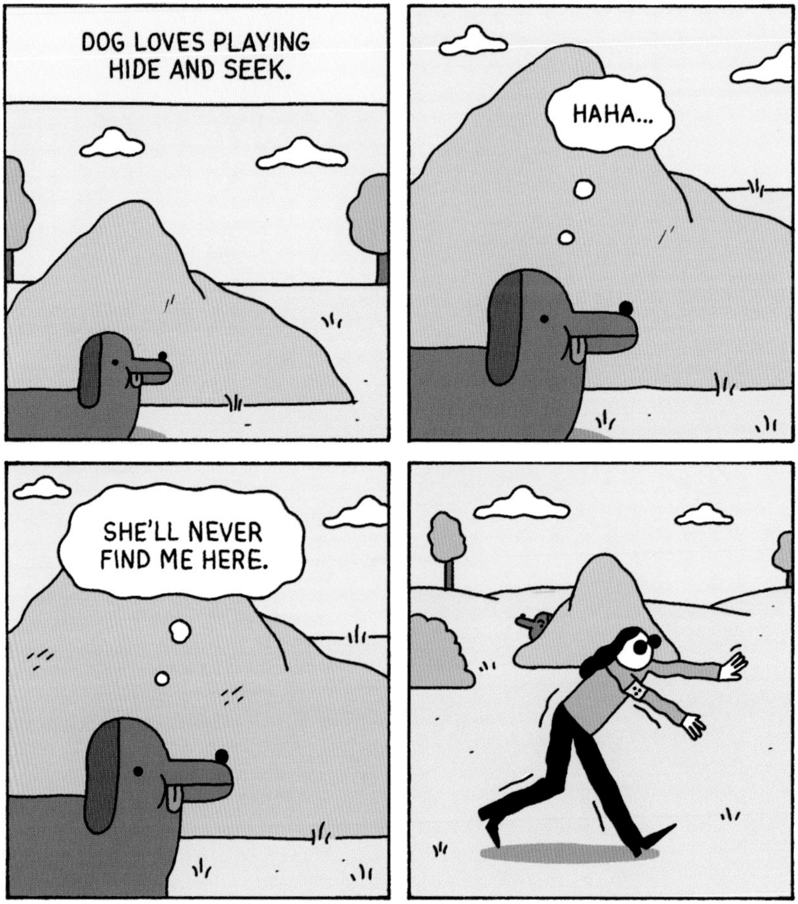
DOG LOVES PLAYING HIDE AND SEEK.
HAHA...
SHE'LL NEVER FIND ME HERE.

NOW WHAT?

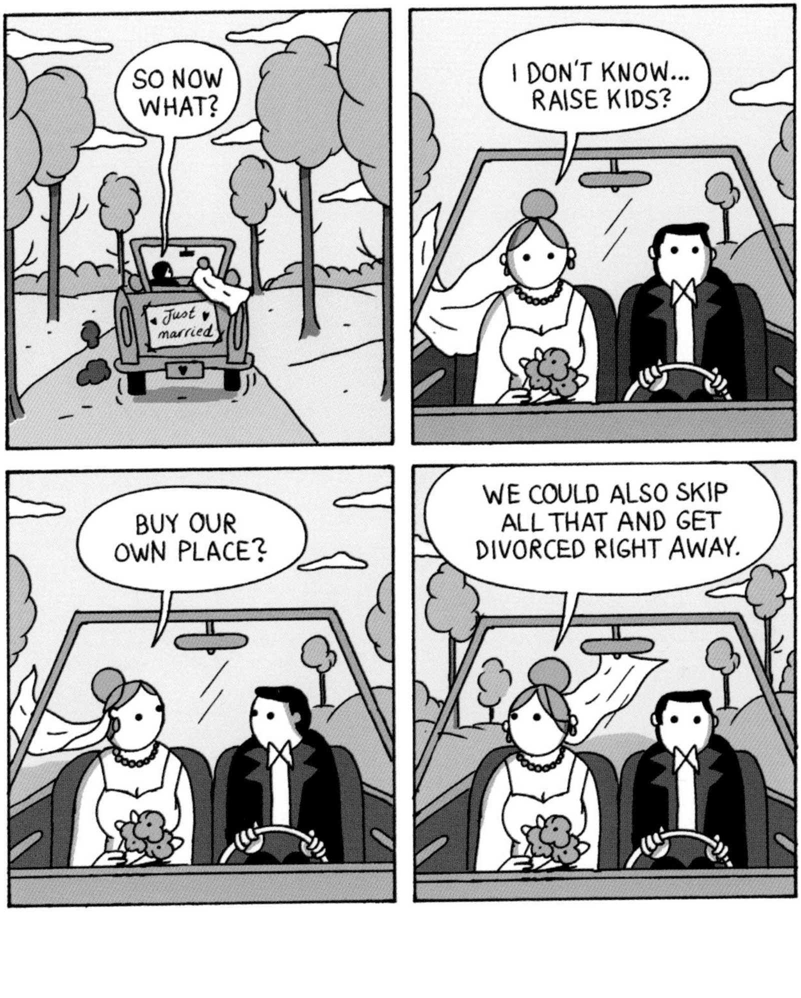

Just married
SO NOW WHAT?
I DON'T KNOW... RAISE KIDS?
BUY OUR OWN PLACE?
WE COULD ALSO SKIP ALL THAT AND GET DIVORCED RIGHT AWAY.

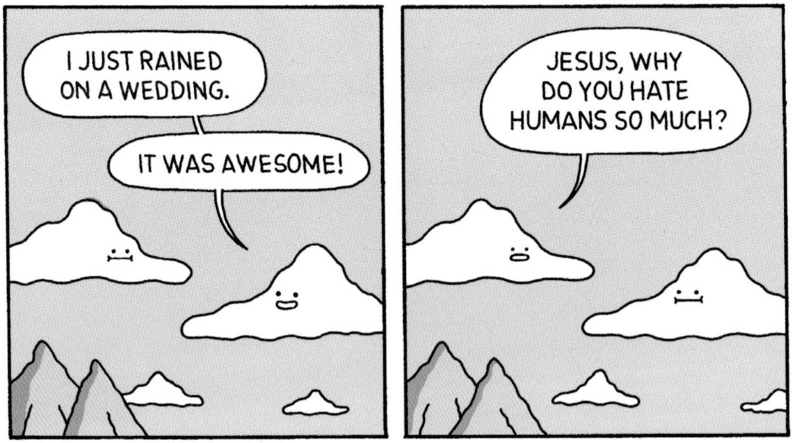
I JUST RAINED ON A WEDDING.
IT WAS AWESOME!
JESUS, WHY DO YOU HATE HUMANS SO MUCH?

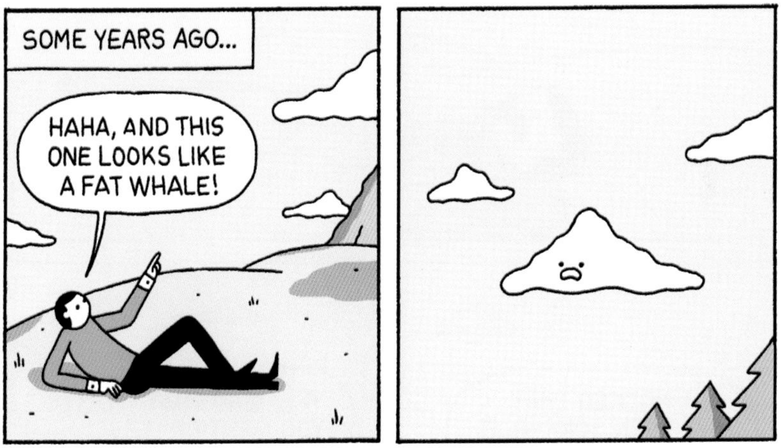
SOME YEARS AGO...
HAHA, AND THIS ONE LOOKS LIKE A FAT WHALE!

MEDITATION

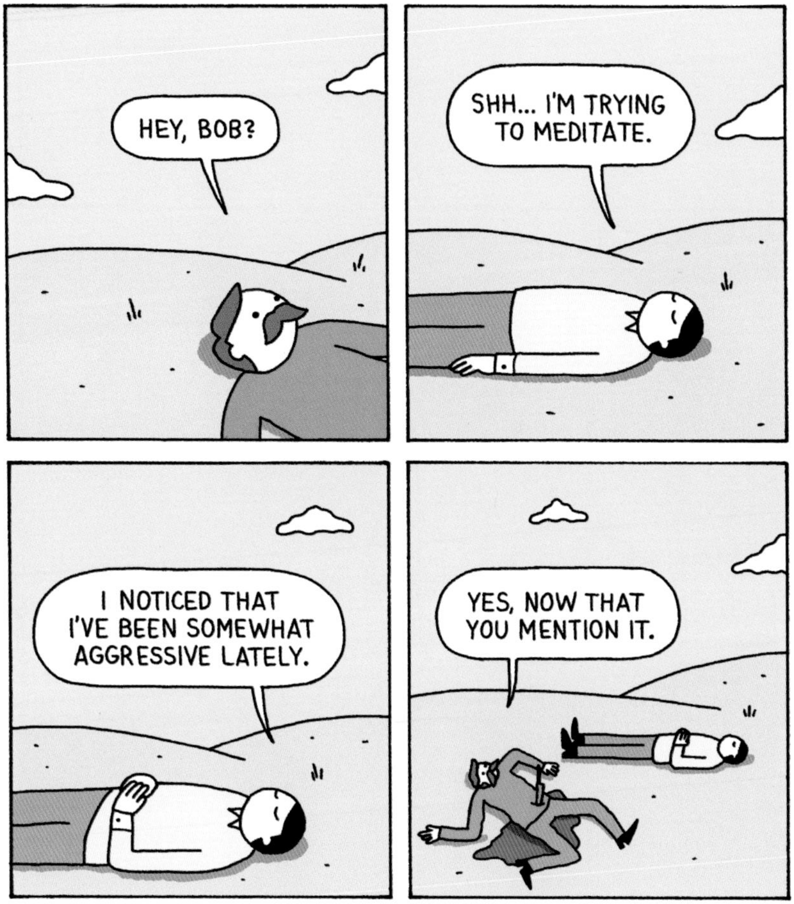

HEY, BOB?
SHH... I'M TRYING TO MEDITATE.
I NOTICED THAT I'VE BEEN SOMEWHAT AGGRESSIVE LATELY.
YES, NOW THAT YOU MENTION IT.

OPPOSITES

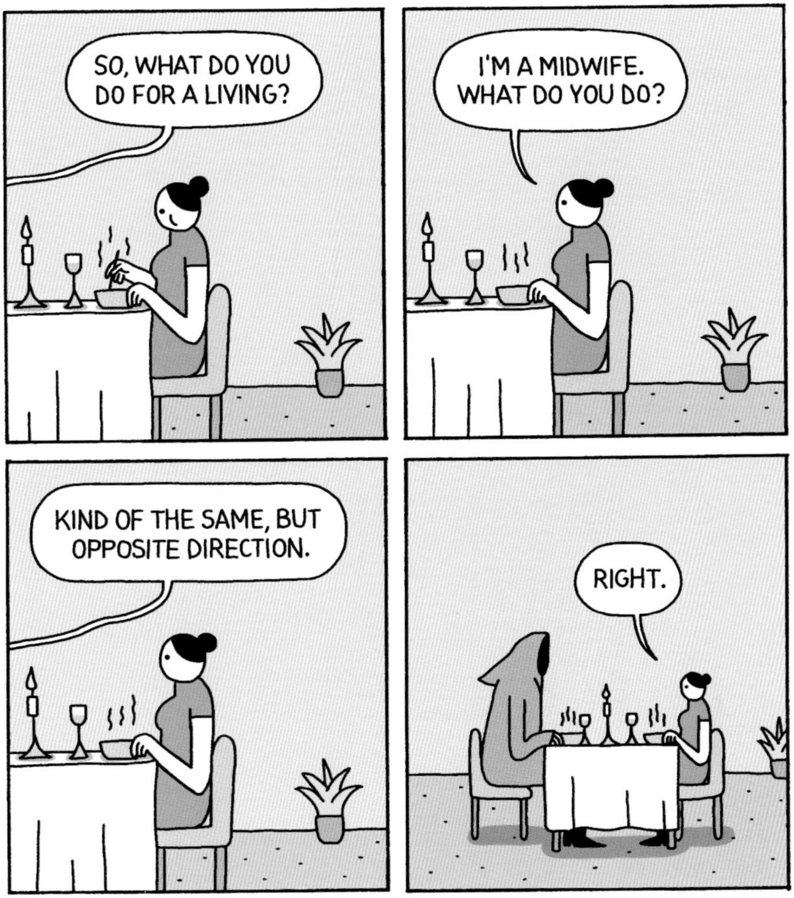
SO, WHAT DO YOU DO FOR A LIVING?
I'M A MIDWIFE. WHAT DO YOU DO?
KIND OF THE SAME, BUT OPPOSITE DIRECTION.
RIGHT.

BEAUTY

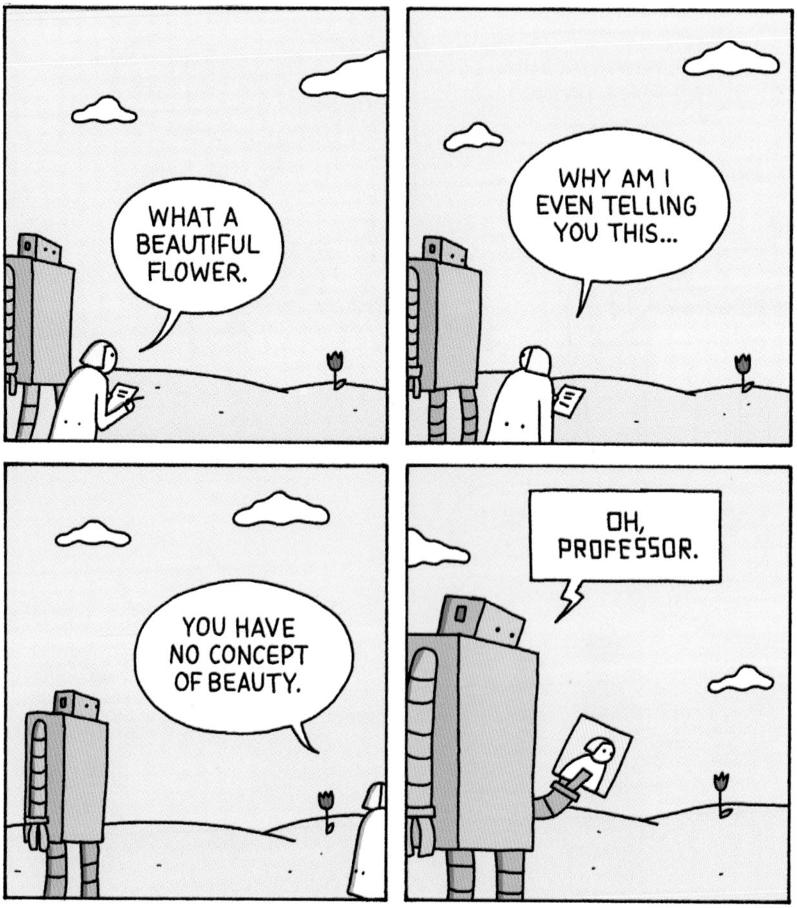

WHAT A BEAUTIFUL FLOWER.
WHY AM I EVEN TELLING YOU THIS...
YOU HAVE NO CONCEPT OF BEAUTY.
OH, PROFESSOR.

HONEYMOON

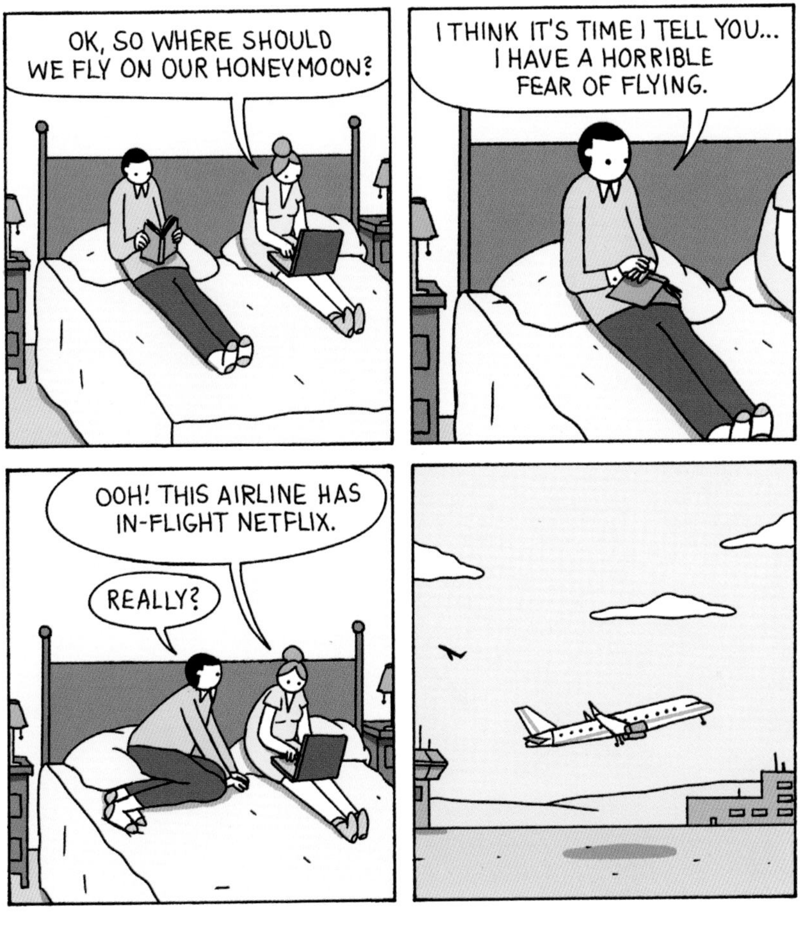
OK, SO WHERE SHOULD WE FLY ON OUR HONEYMOON?
I THINK IT'S TIME I TELL YOU... I HAVE A HORRIBLE FEAR OF FLYING.
OOH! THIS AIRLINE HAS IN-FLIGHT NETFLIX.
REALLY?

KIDS THESE DAYS

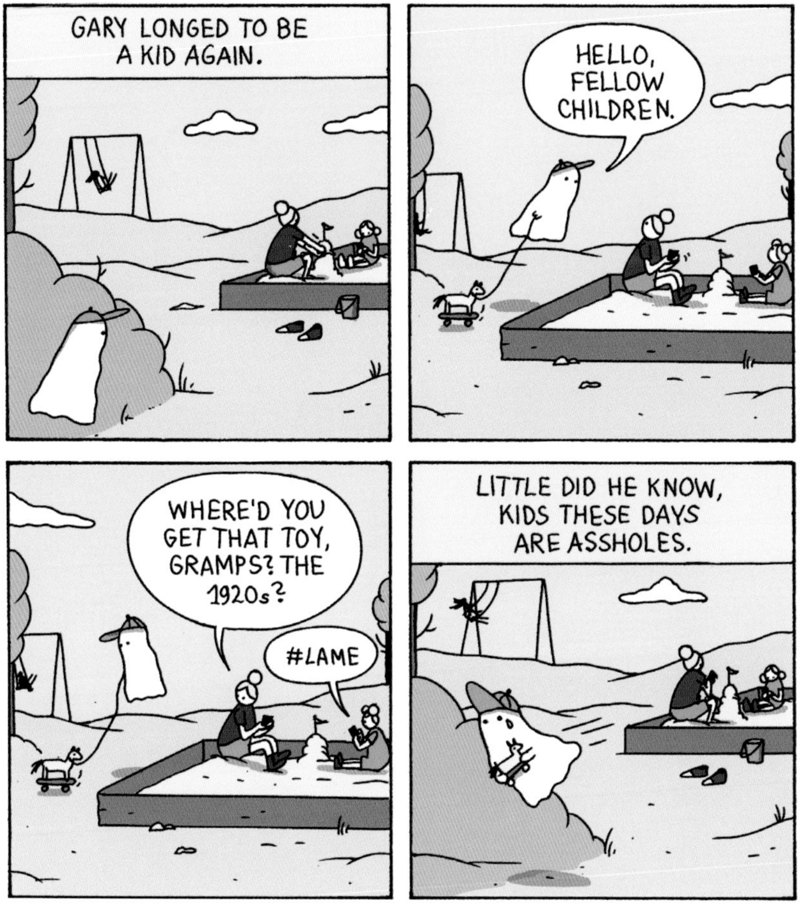
GARY LONGED TO BE A KID AGAIN.
HELLO, FELLOW CHILDREN.
WHERE'D YOU GET THAT TOY, GRAMPS? THE 1920s?
#LAME
LITTLE DID HE KNOW, KIDS THESE DAYS ARE ASSHOLES.

HACKER DOG

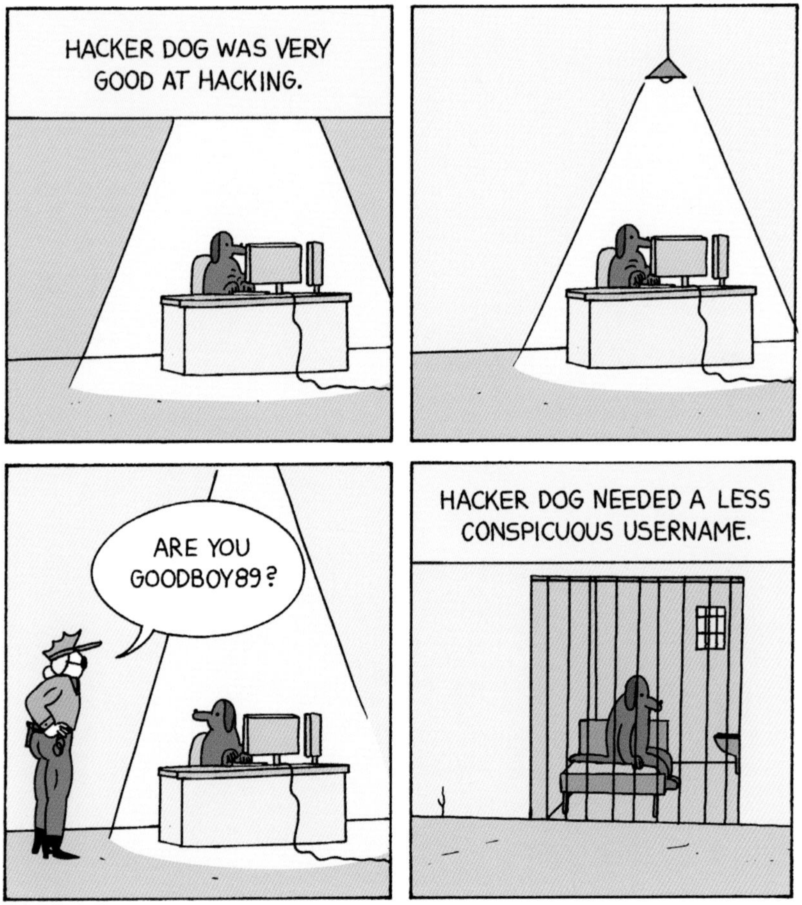
HACKER DOG WAS VERY GOOD AT HACKING.
ARE YOU GOODBOY89?
HACKER DOG NEEDED A LESS CONSPICUOUS USERNAME.

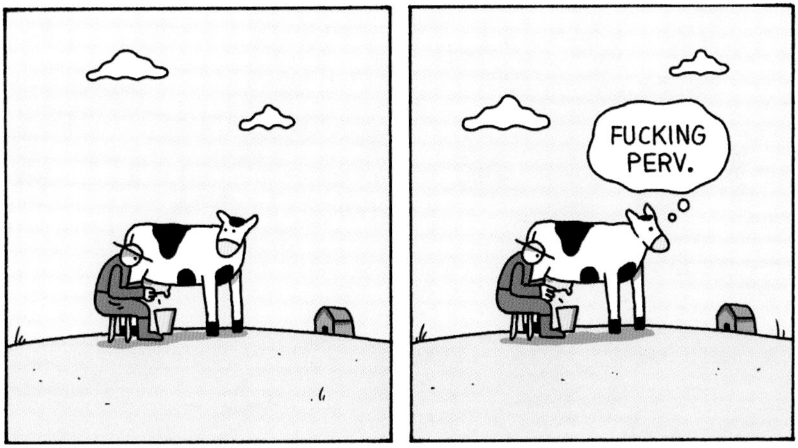
FUCKING
PERV.

CUTE BABY

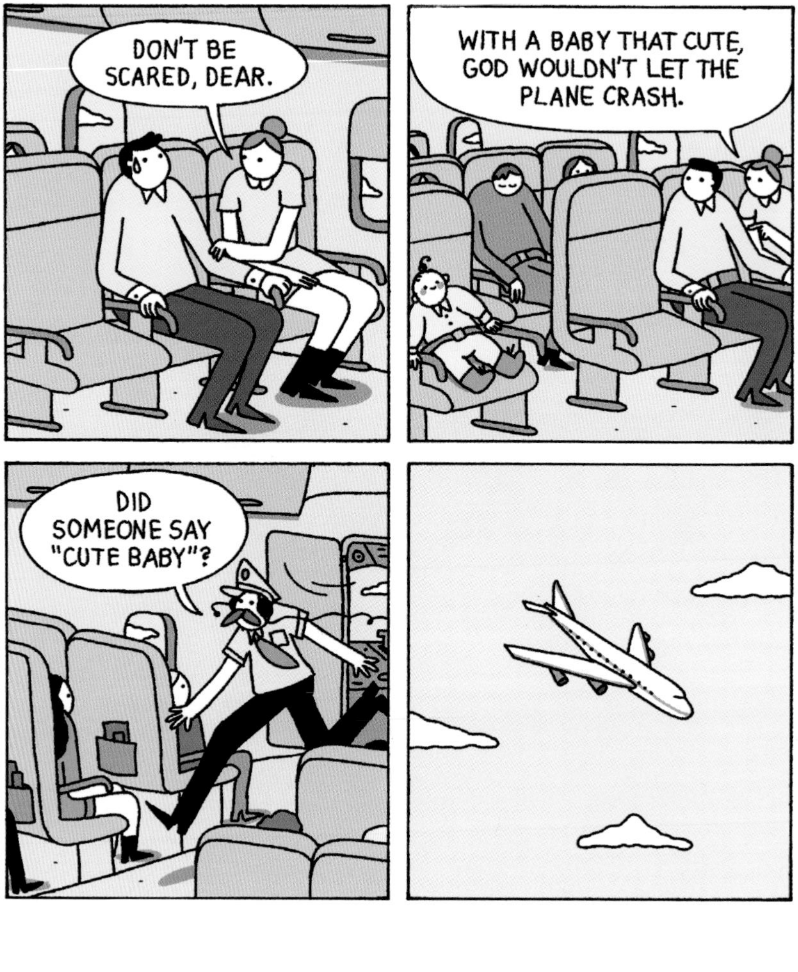
DON'T BE SCARED, DEAR.
WITH A BABY THAT CUTE, GOD WOULDN'T LET THE PLANE CRASH.
DID SOMEONE SAY "CUTE BABY"?

GOING OUT

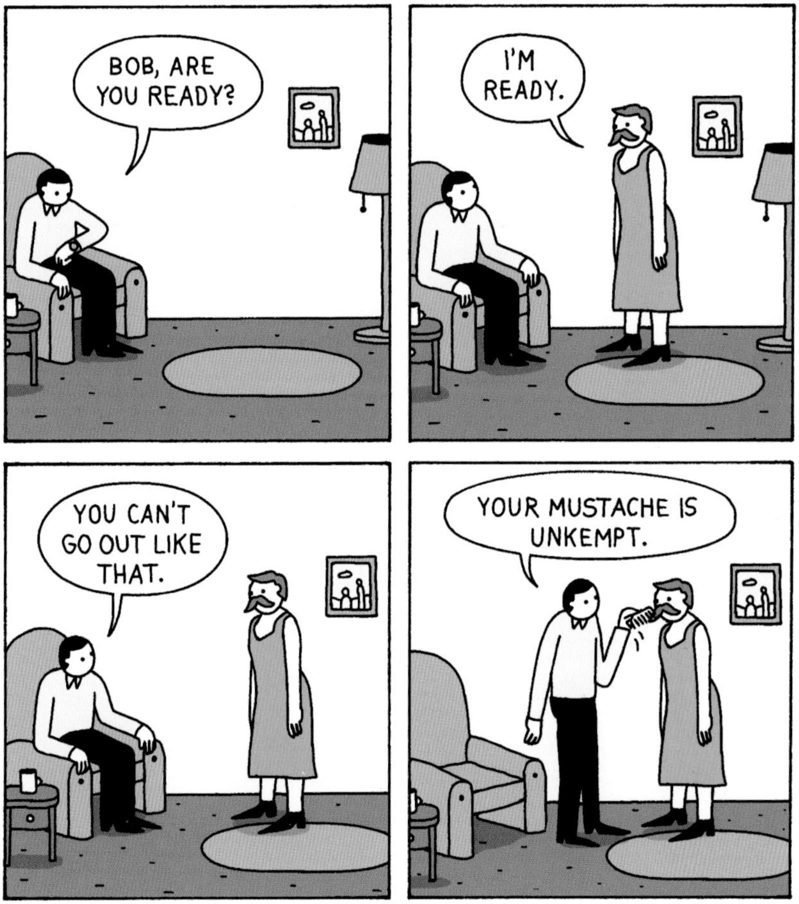
BOB, ARE YOU READY?
I'M READY.
YOU CAN'T GO OUT LIKE THAT.
YOUR MUSTACHE IS UNKEMPT.

NOT LIKE THIS

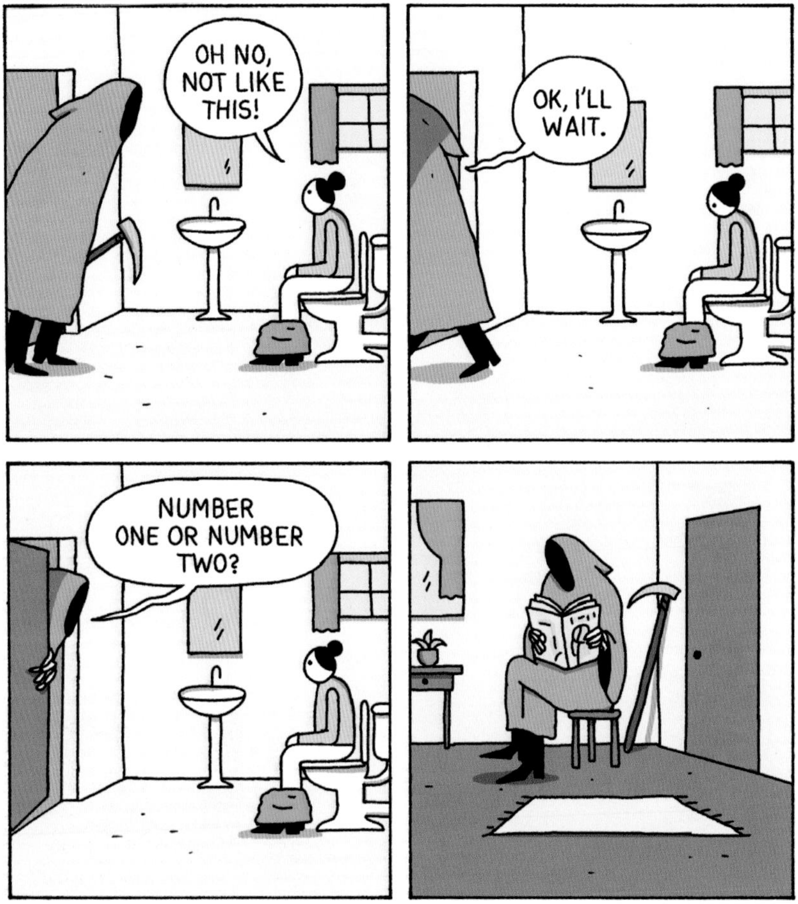
OH NO, NOT LIKE THIS!
OK, I'LL WAIT.
NUMBER ONE OR NUMBER TWO?

FASCINATING

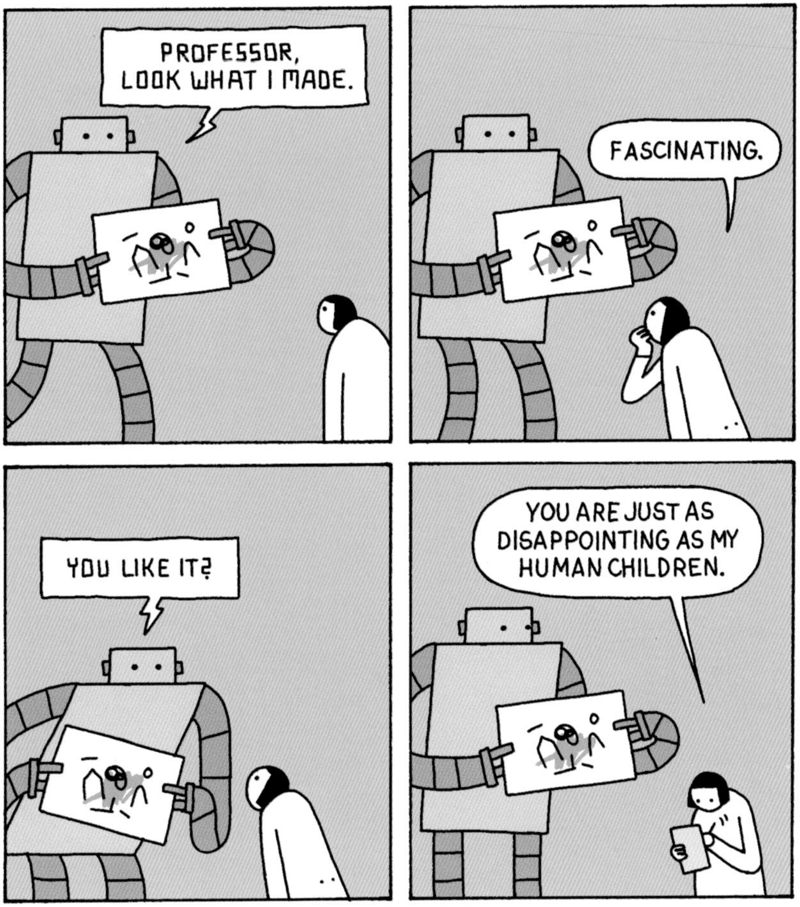
PROFESSOR, LOOK WHAT I MADE.
FASCINATING.
YOU LIKE IT?
YOU ARE JUST AS DISAPPOINTING AS MY HUMAN CHILDREN.

BLINK

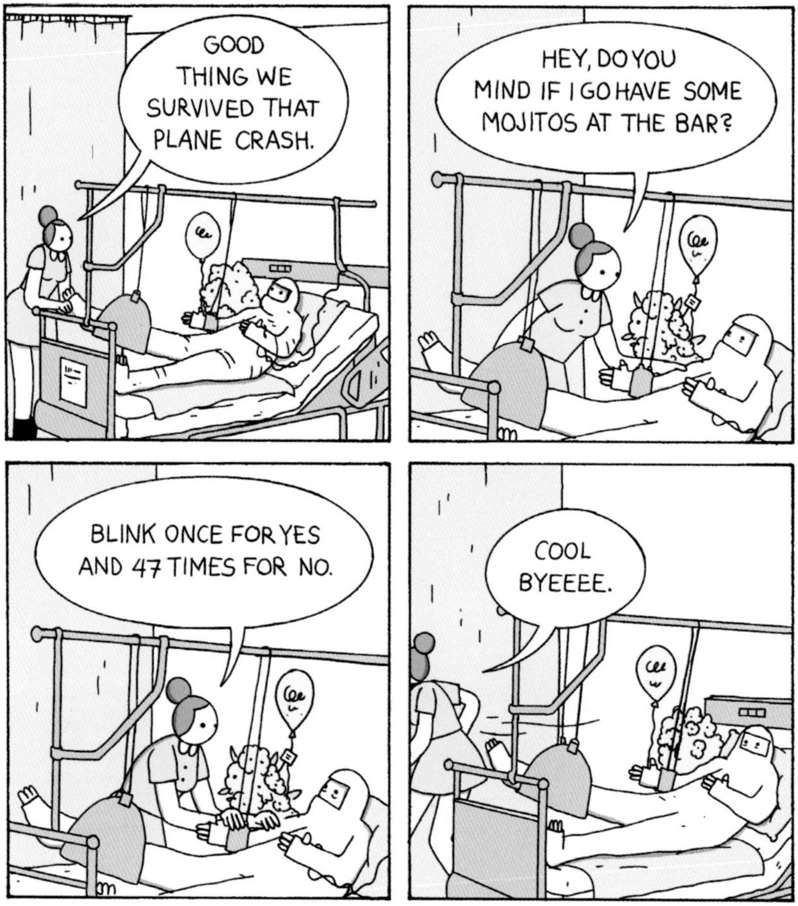
GOOD THING WE SURVIVED THAT PLANE CRASH.
HEY, DO YOU MIND IF I GO HAVE SOME MOJITOS AT THE BAR?
BLINK ONCE FOR YES AND 47 TIMES FOR NO.
COOL BYEEEE.

LITERALLY

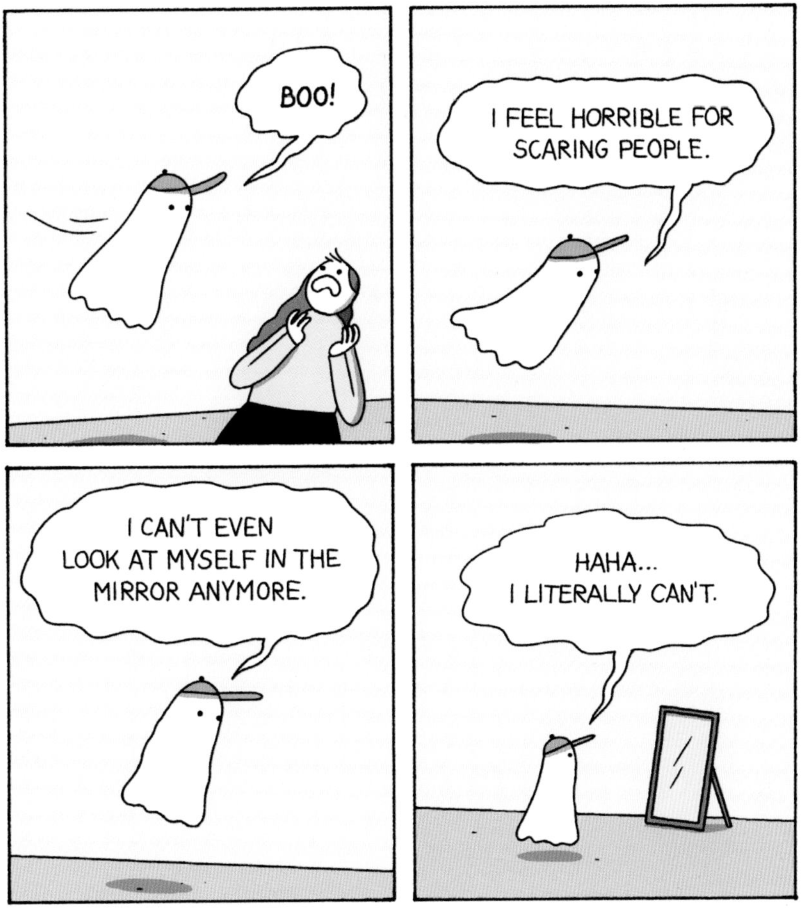
BOO!
I FEEL HORRIBLE FOR SCARING PEOPLE.
I CAN'T EVEN LOOK AT MYSELF IN THE MIRROR ANYMORE.
HAHA... I LITERALLY CAN'T.

A.C.A.B.

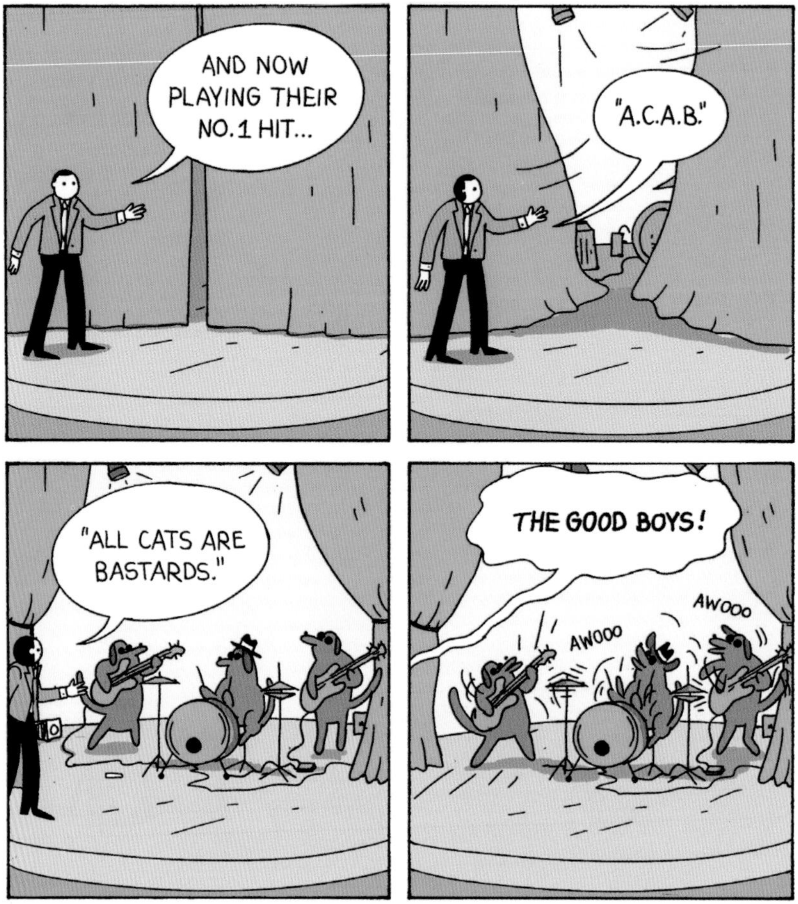
AND NOW PLAYING THEIR NO. 1 HIT...
"A.C.A.B."
"ALL CATS ARE BASTARDS."
THE GOOD BOYS!
AWOOO
AWOOO

RESPECT

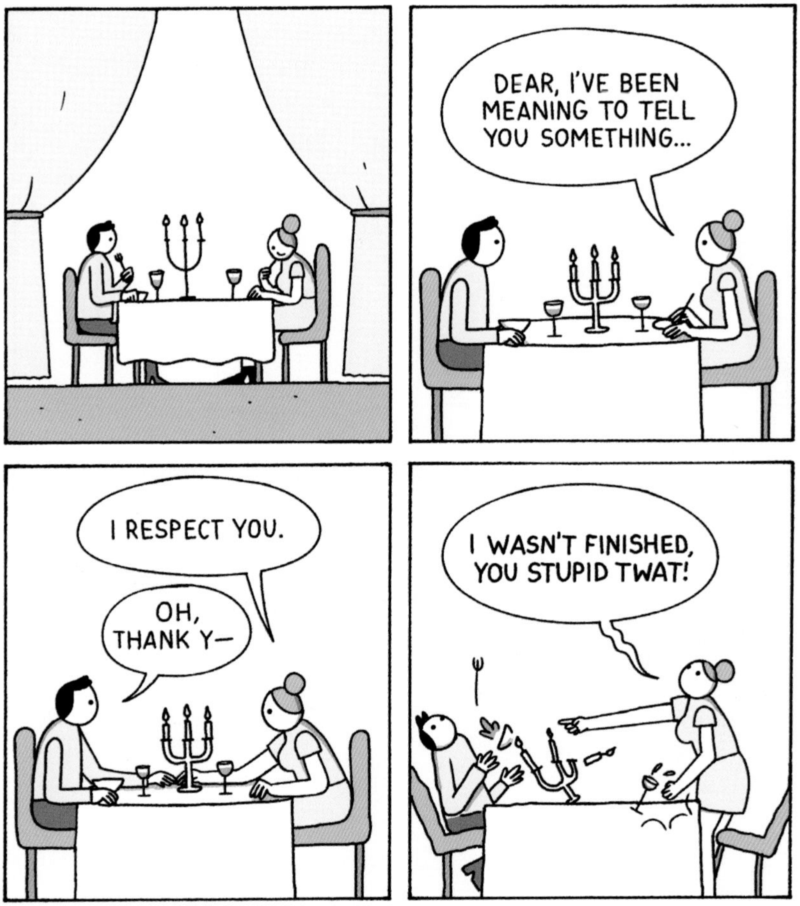

DEAR, I'VE BEEN MEANING TO TELL YOU SOMETHING...
I RESPECT YOU.
OH, THANK Y—
I WASN'T FINISHED, YOU STUPID TWAT!

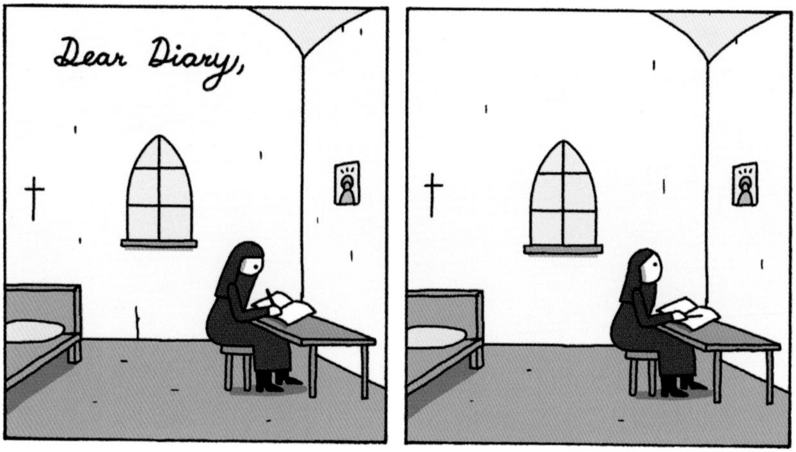
Dear Diary,

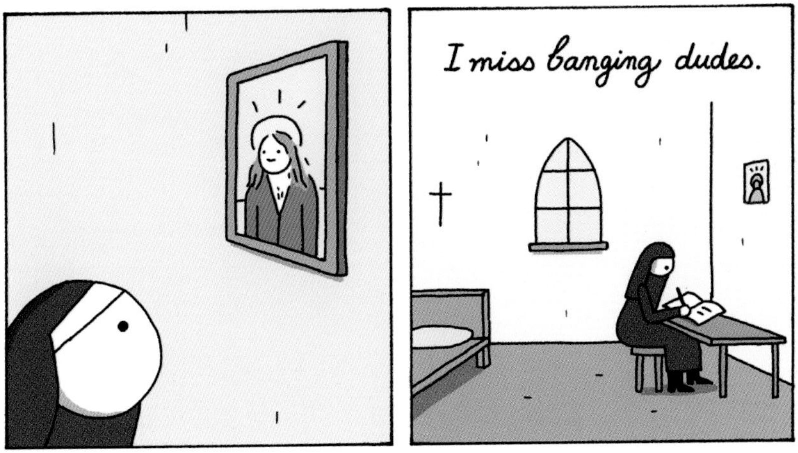
I miss banging dudes.

I KNOW

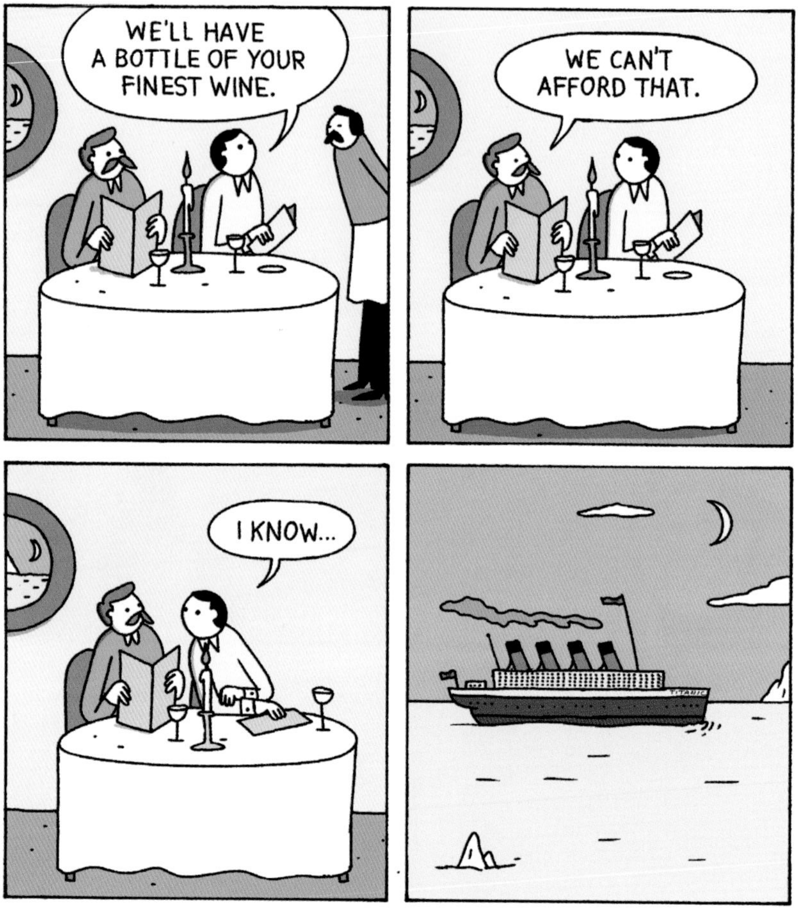

WE'LL HAVE A BOTTLE OF YOUR FINEST WINE.
WE CAN'T AFFORD THAT.
I KNOW...

DELICIOUS BONES

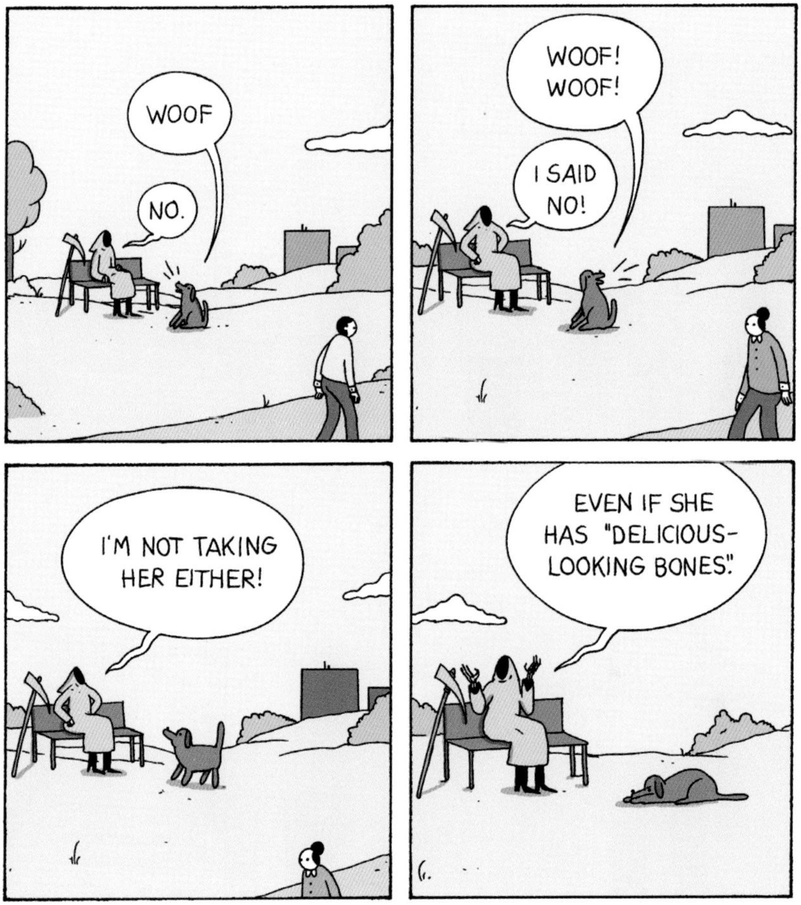
WOOF
NO.
WOOF! WOOF!
I SAID NO!
I'M NOT TAKING HER EITHER!
EVEN IF SHE HAS "DELICIOUS-LOOKING BONES."

WHAT IS LOVE?

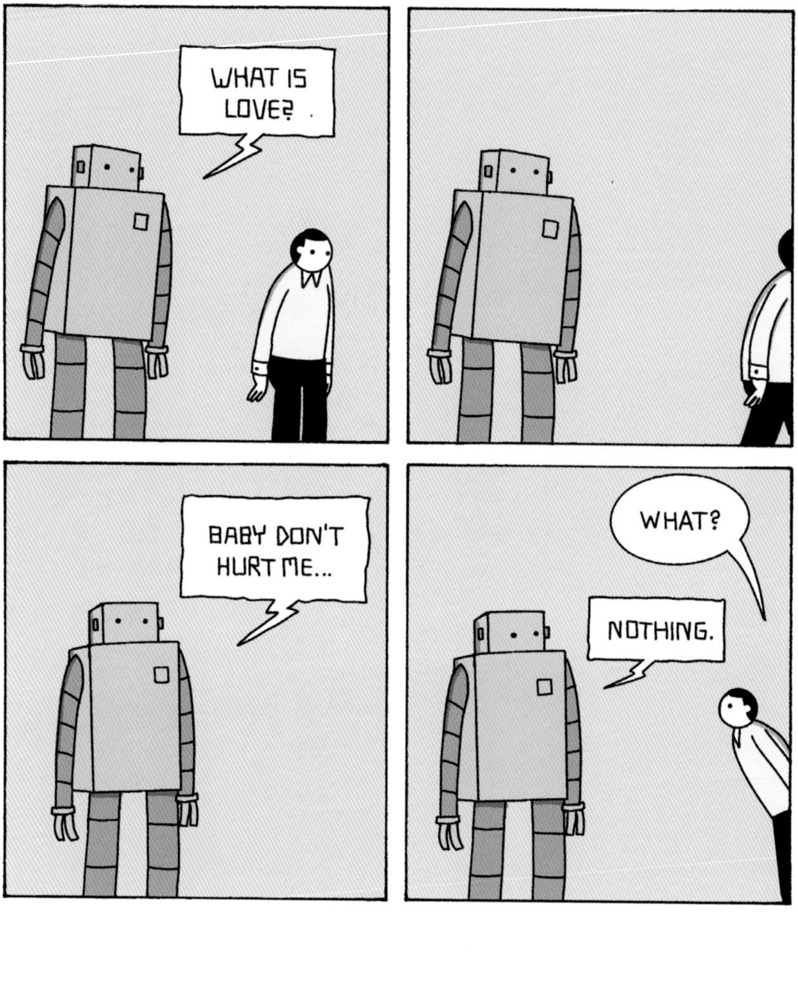
WHAT IS LOVE?
BABY DON'T HURT ME...
WHAT?
NOTHING.

Z-DAY

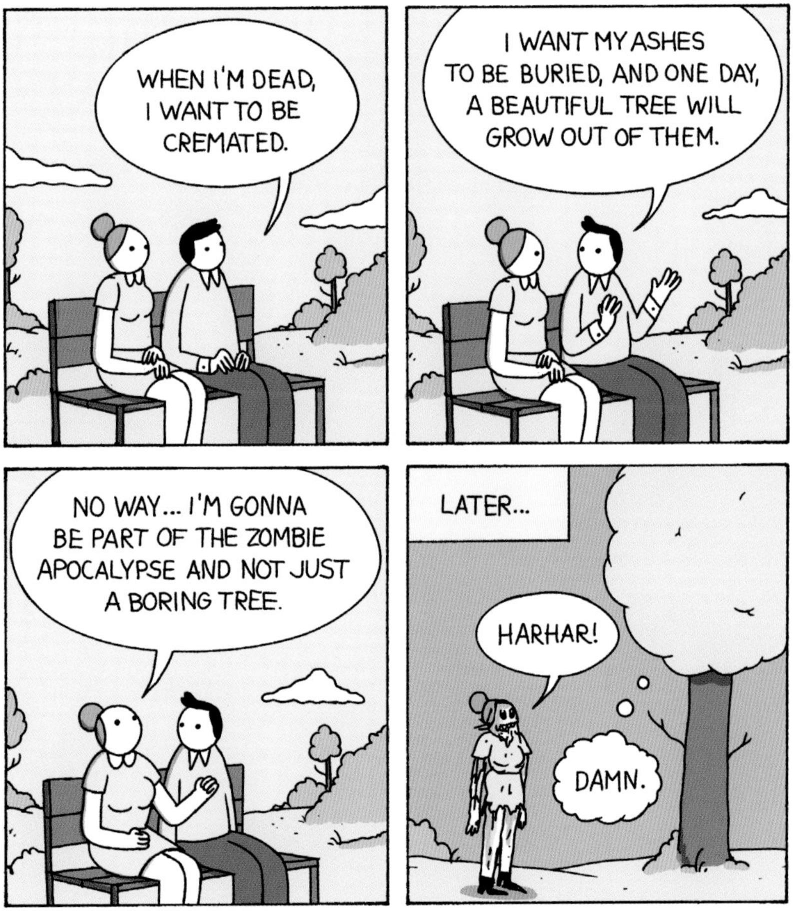

WHEN I'M DEAD, I WANT TO BE CREMATED.
I WANT MY ASHES TO BE BURIED, AND ONE DAY, A BEAUTIFUL TREE WILL GROW OUT OF THEM.
NO WAY... I'M GONNA BE PART OF THE ZOMBIE APOCALYPSE AND NOT JUST A BORING TREE.
LATER...
HARHAR!
DAMN.

POSSESSION 101

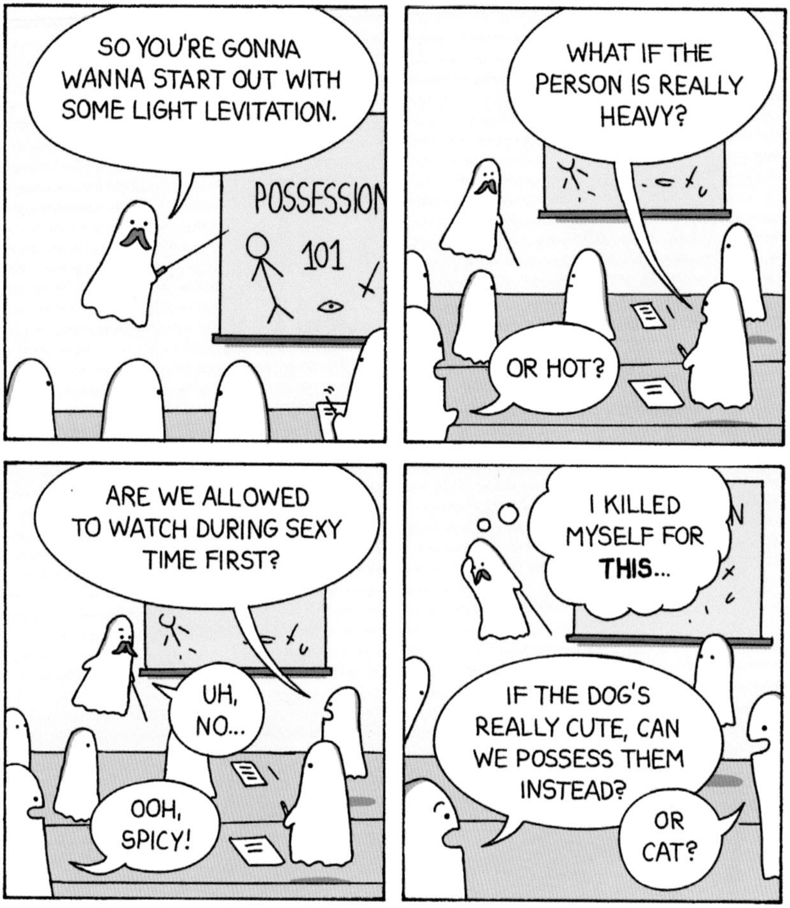
SO YOU'RE GONNA WANNA START OUT WITH SOME LIGHT LEVITATION.
POSSESSION 101
WHAT IF THE PERSON IS REALLY HEAVY?
OR HOT?
ARE WE ALLOWED TO WATCH DURING SEXY TIME FIRST?
UH, NO...
OOH, SPICY!
I KILLED MYSELF FOR **THIS**...
IF THE DOG'S REALLY CUTE, CAN WE POSSESS THEM INSTEAD?
OR CAT?

LIFE OF DOG

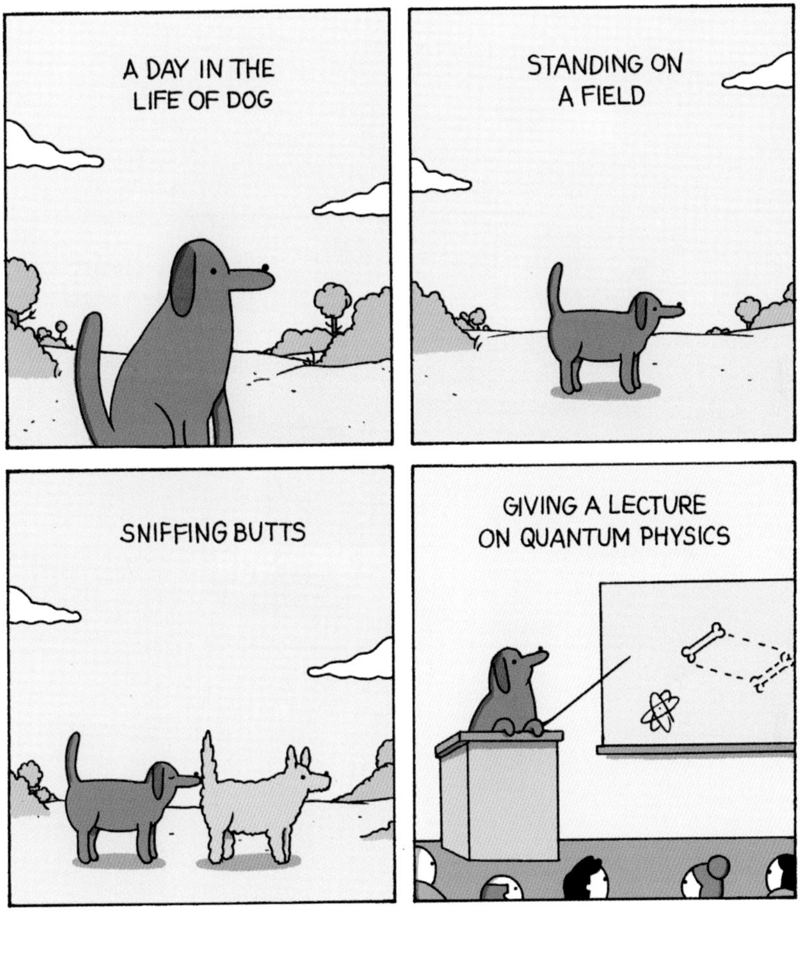
A DAY IN THE
LIFE OF DOG
STANDING ON
A FIELD
SNIFFING BUTTS
GIVING A LECTURE
ON QUANTUM PHYSICS

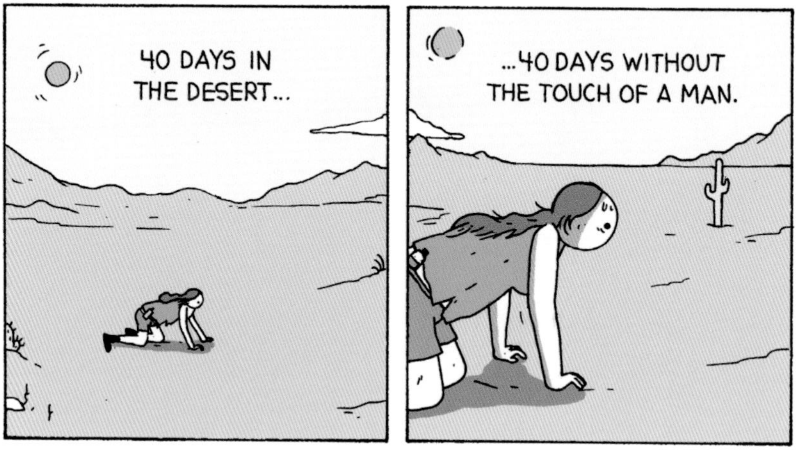
40 DAYS IN THE DESERT...
...40 DAYS WITHOUT THE TOUCH OF A MAN.

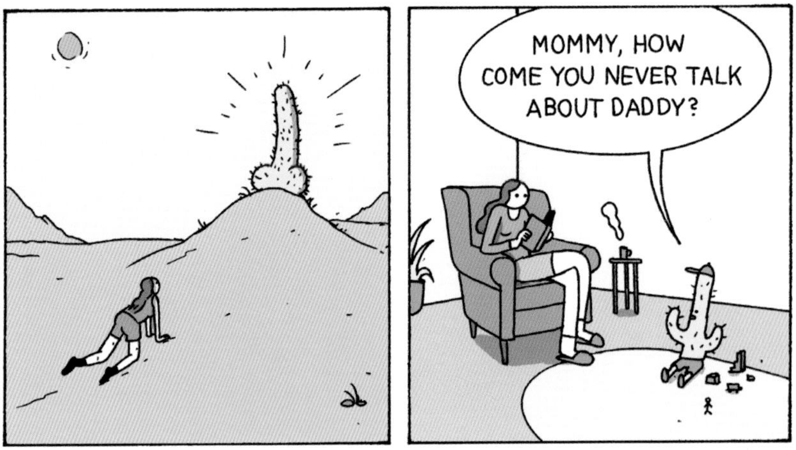
MOMMY, HOW COME YOU NEVER TALK ABOUT DADDY?

PRETTY SURE

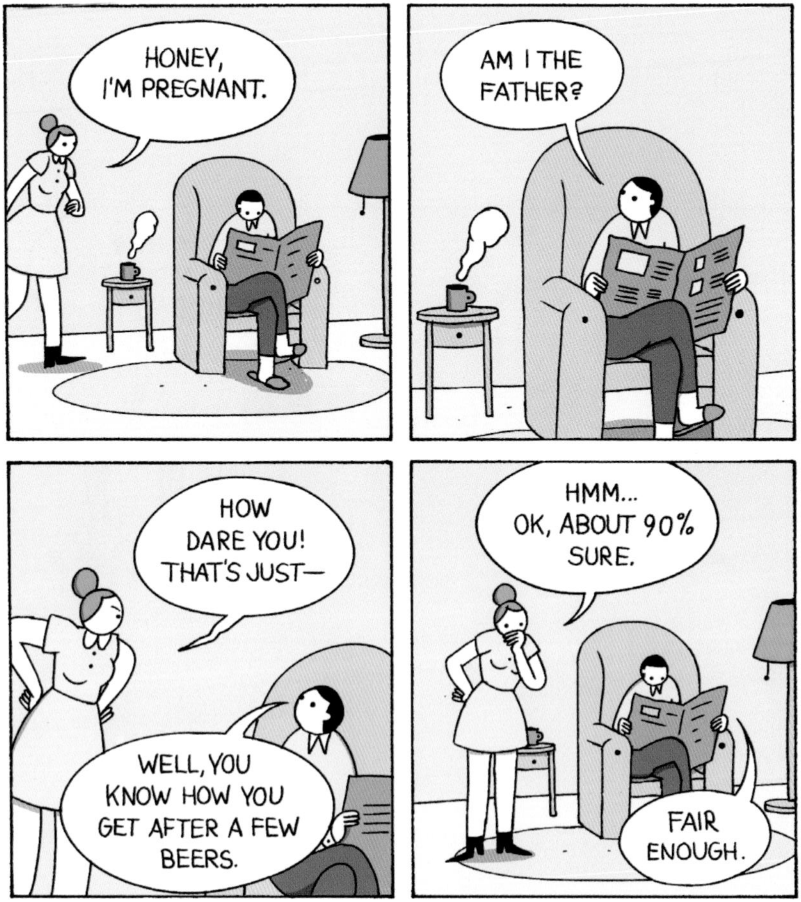

HONEY, I'M PREGNANT.
AM I THE FATHER?
HOW DARE YOU! THAT'S JUST—
WELL, YOU KNOW HOW YOU GET AFTER A FEW BEERS.
HMM... OK, ABOUT 90% SURE.
FAIR ENOUGH.

NATURAL-BORN LEADER

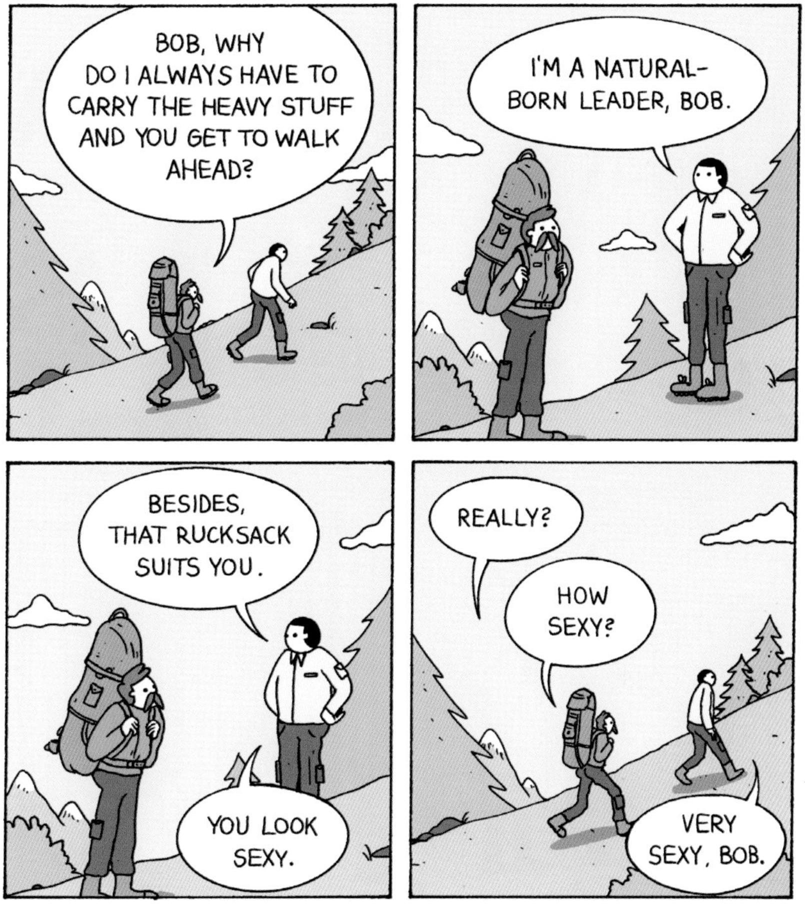

BOB, WHY DO I ALWAYS HAVE TO CARRY THE HEAVY STUFF AND YOU GET TO WALK AHEAD?
I'M A NATURAL-BORN LEADER, BOB.
BESIDES, THAT RUCKSACK SUITS YOU.
YOU LOOK SEXY.
REALLY?
HOW SEXY?
VERY SEXY, BOB.

REJUVENATING

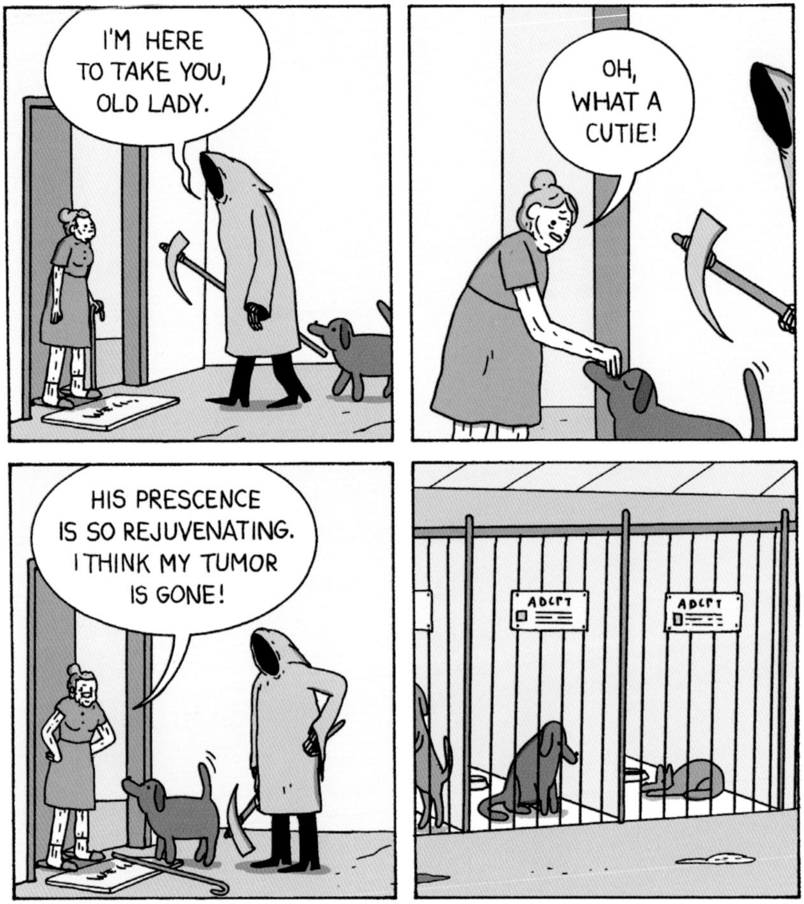
I'M HERE TO TAKE YOU, OLD LADY.
OH, WHAT A CUTIE!
HIS PRESCENCE IS SO REJUVENATING. I THINK MY TUMOR IS GONE!

EMPOWERMENT MODULE

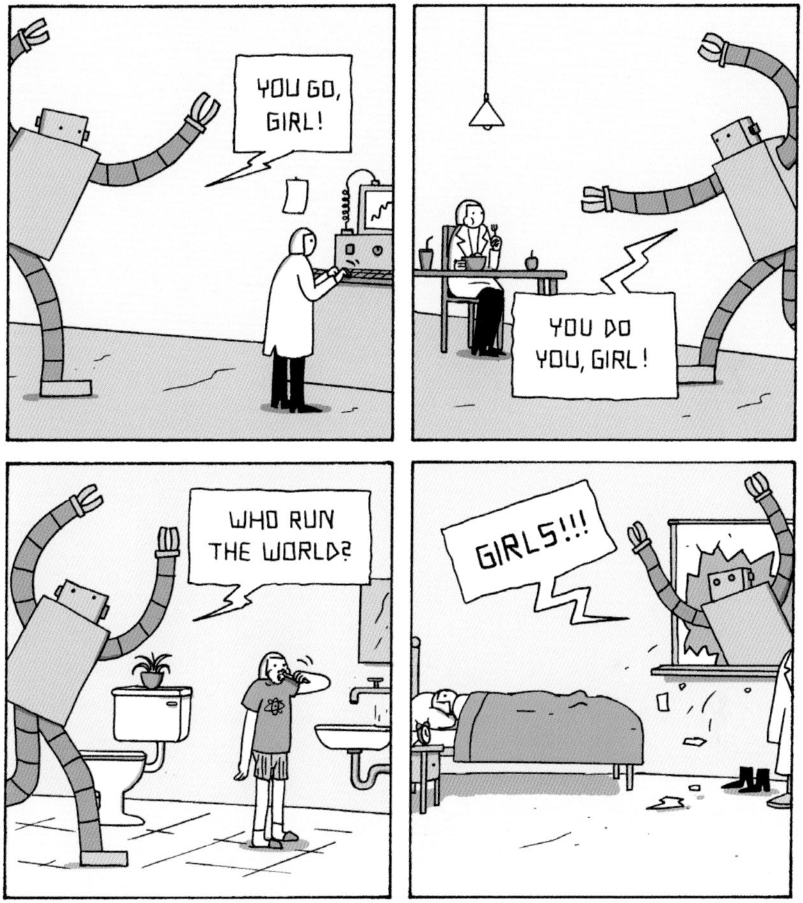

YOU GO, GIRL!
YOU DO YOU, GIRL!
WHO RUN THE WORLD?
GIRLS!!!

SO LAME

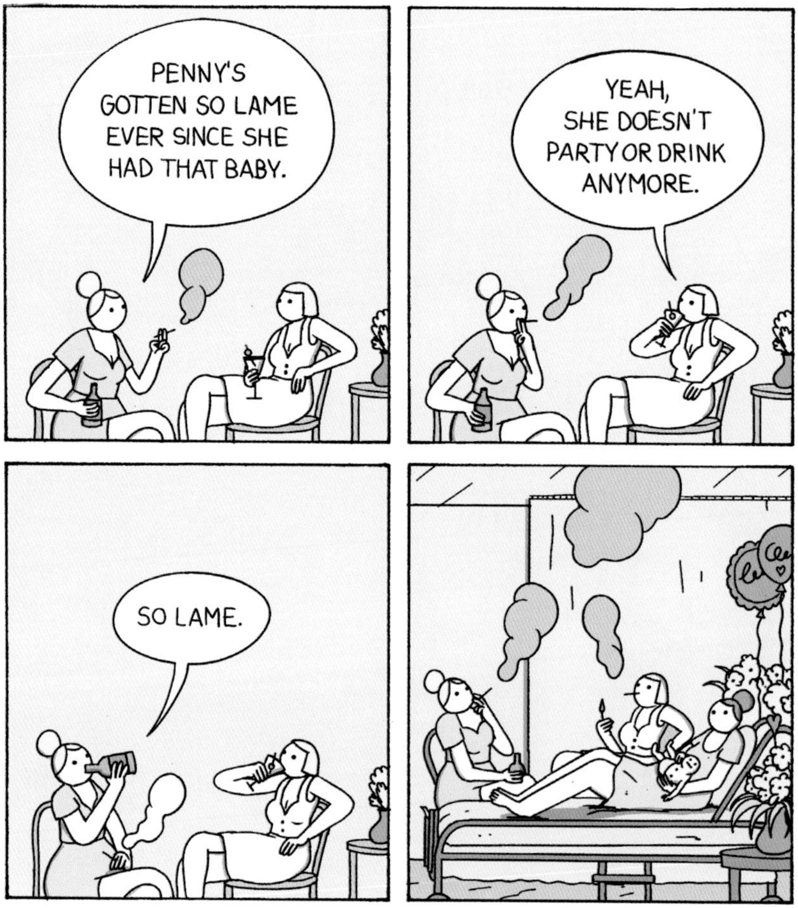

PENNY'S GOTTEN SO LAME EVER SINCE SHE HAD THAT BABY.
YEAH, SHE DOESN'T PARTY OR DRINK ANYMORE.
SO LAME.

I HAVE FRIENDS

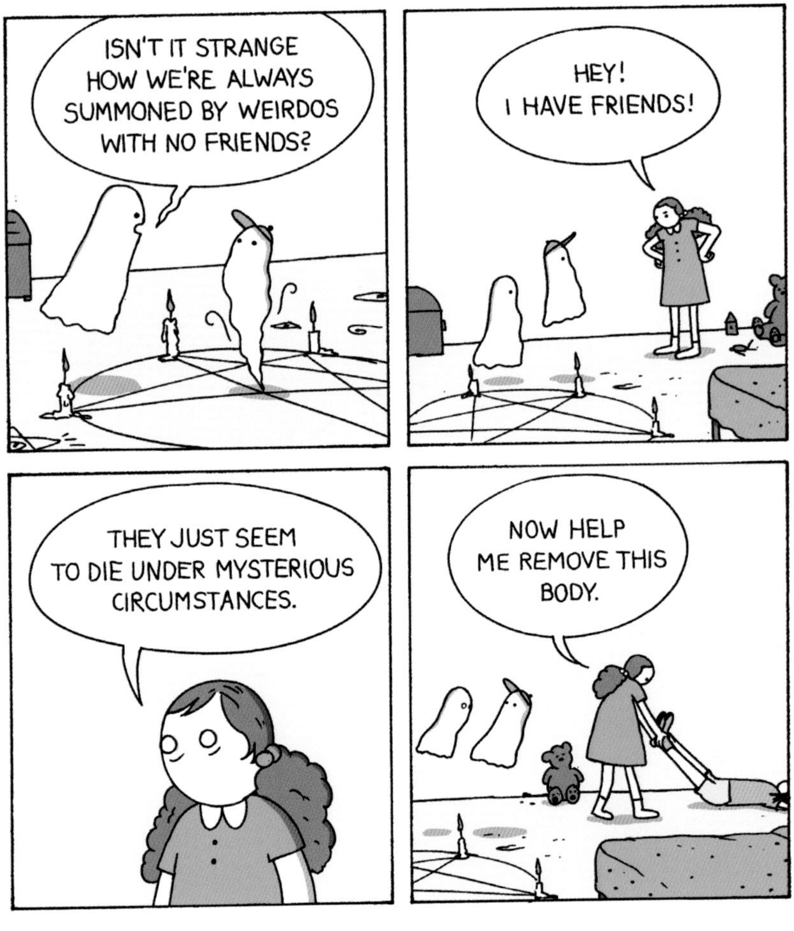

ISN'T IT STRANGE HOW WE'RE ALWAYS SUMMONED BY WEIRDOS WITH NO FRIENDS?
HEY! I HAVE FRIENDS!
THEY JUST SEEM TO DIE UNDER MYSTERIOUS CIRCUMSTANCES.
NOW HELP ME REMOVE THIS BODY.

INTO THE WILD

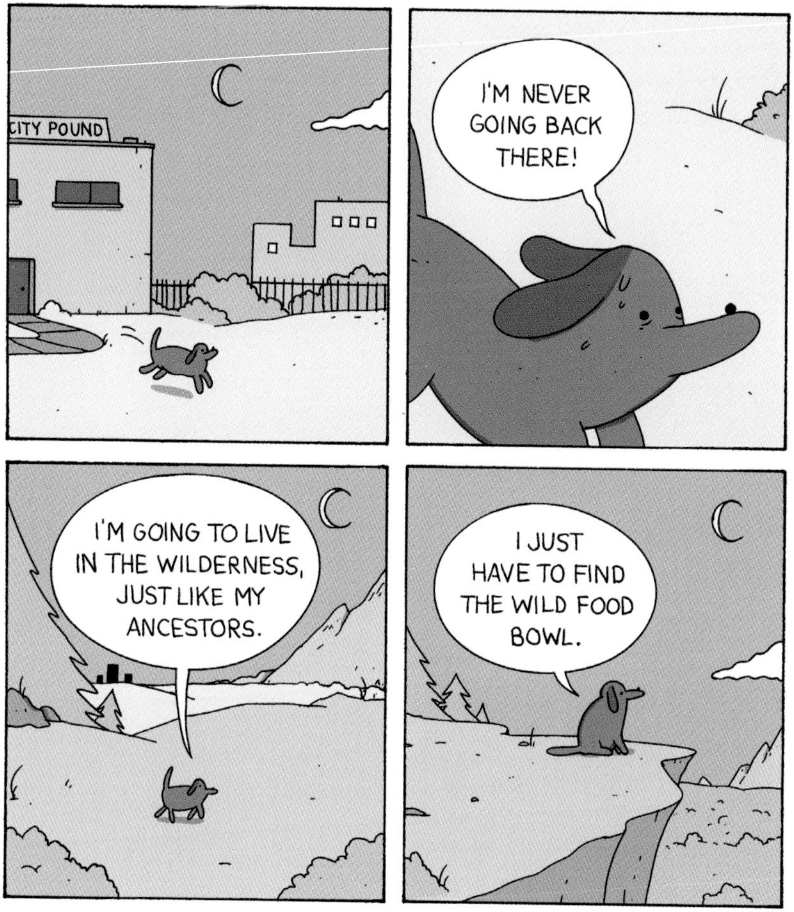
CITY POUND
I'M NEVER GOING BACK THERE!
I'M GOING TO LIVE IN THE WILDERNESS, JUST LIKE MY ANCESTORS.
I JUST HAVE TO FIND THE WILD FOOD BOWL.

FUNNY COMIC

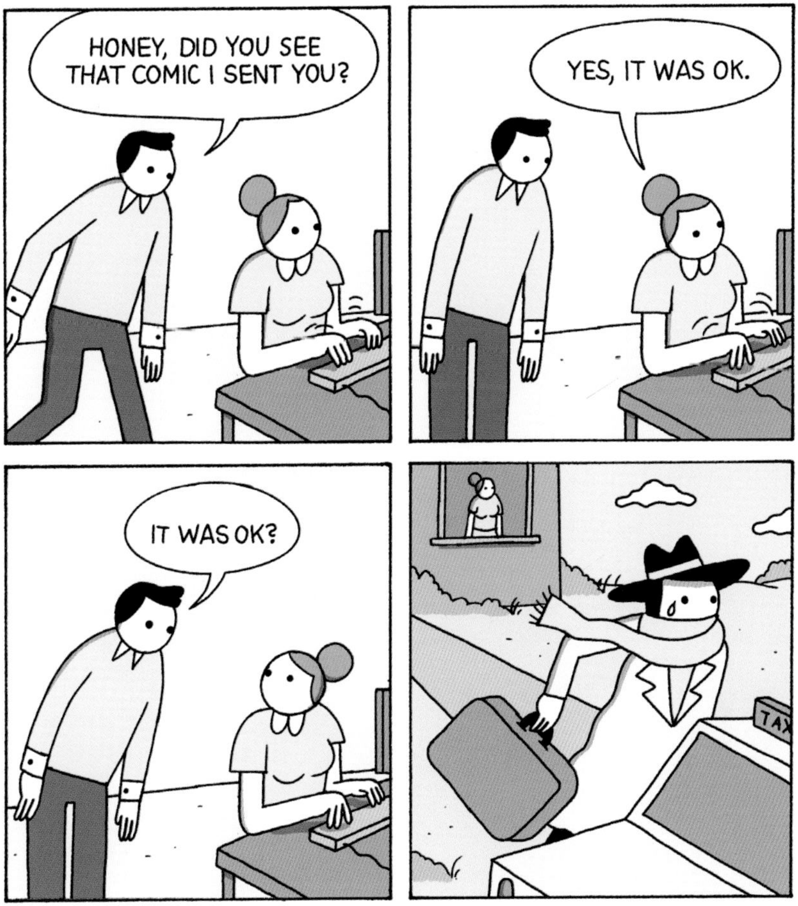
HONEY, DID YOU SEE THAT COMIC I SENT YOU?
YES, IT WAS OK.
IT WAS OK?
TAX

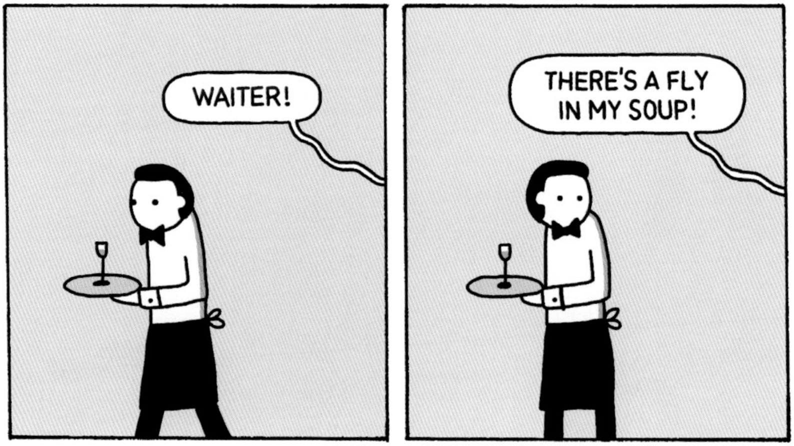
WAITER!
THERE'S A FLY IN MY SOUP!

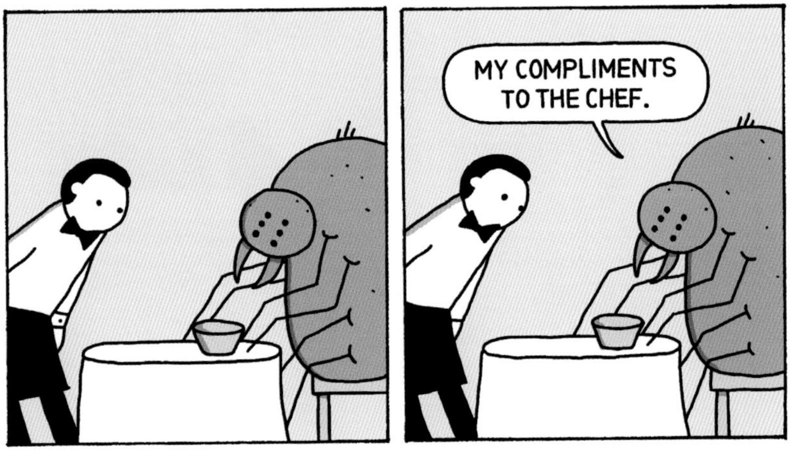
MY COMPLIMENTS TO THE CHEF.

THE DOCTOR

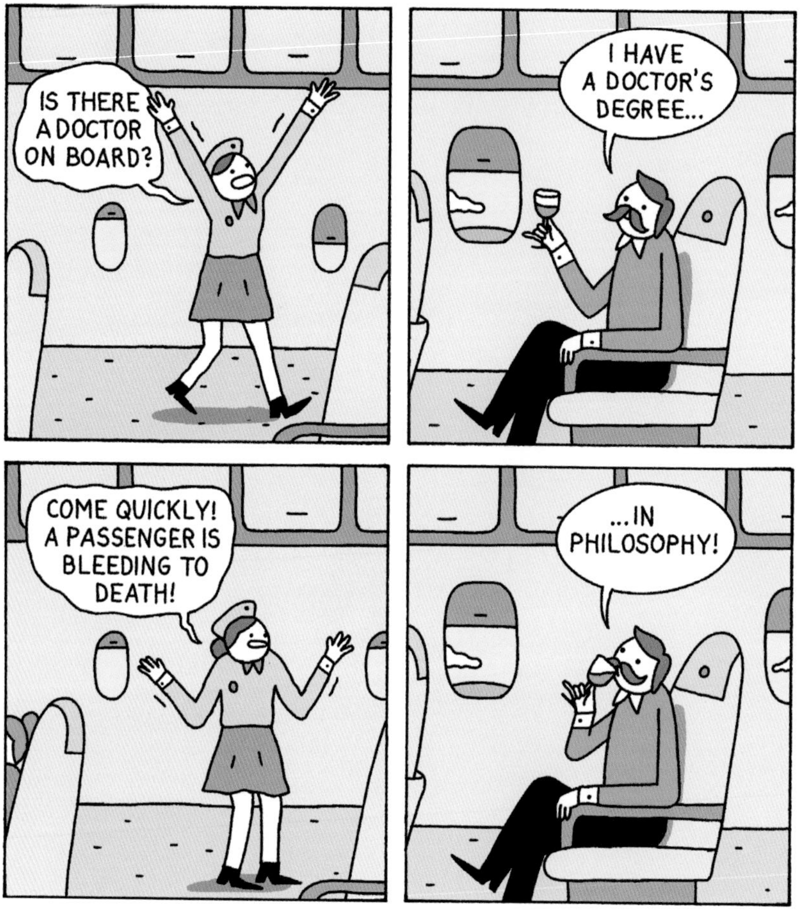
IS THERE A DOCTOR ON BOARD?
I HAVE A DOCTOR'S DEGREE...
COME QUICKLY! A PASSENGER IS BLEEDING TO DEATH!
...IN PHILOSOPHY!

BEAUTIFUL SADNESS

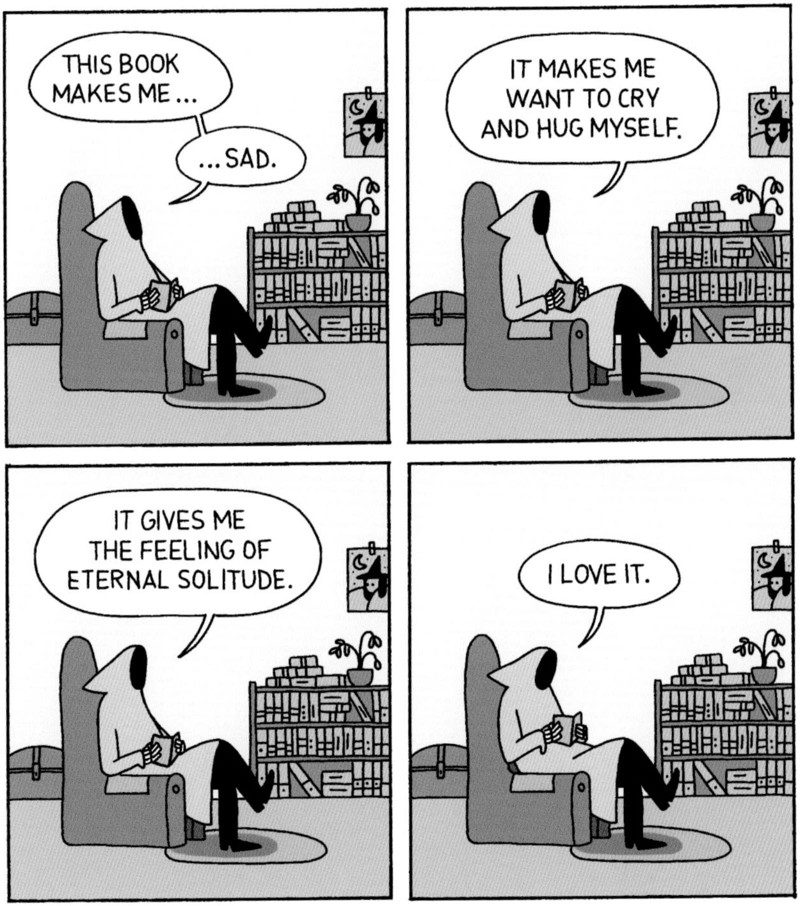
THIS BOOK MAKES ME ...
... SAD.
IT MAKES ME WANT TO CRY AND HUG MYSELF.
IT GIVES ME THE FEELING OF ETERNAL SOLITUDE.
I LOVE IT.

MR. ROBOTO

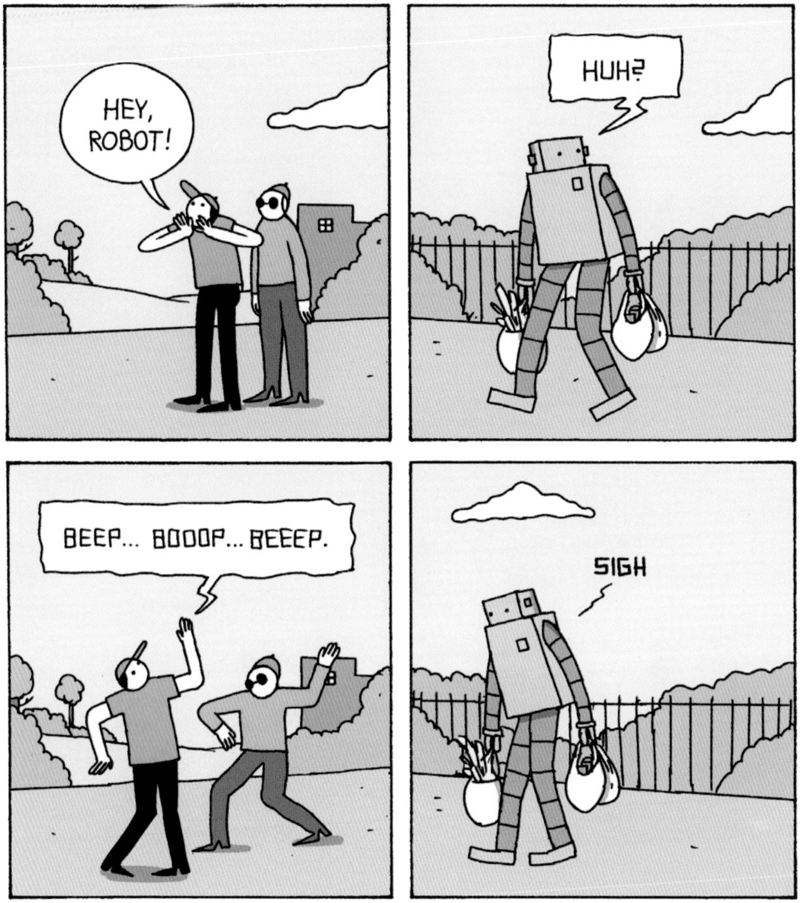
HEY, ROBOT!
HUH?
BEEP... BOOOP... BEEEP.
SIGH

SOULMATES

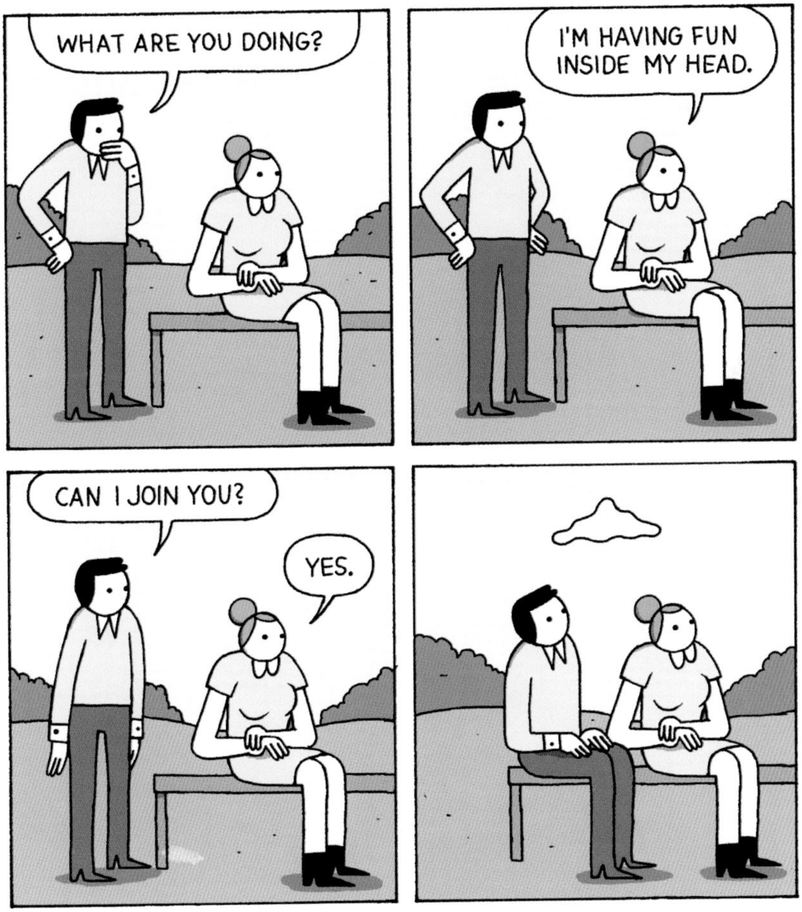
WHAT ARE YOU DOING?
I'M HAVING FUN INSIDE MY HEAD.
CAN I JOIN YOU?
YES.

ELECTRICITY

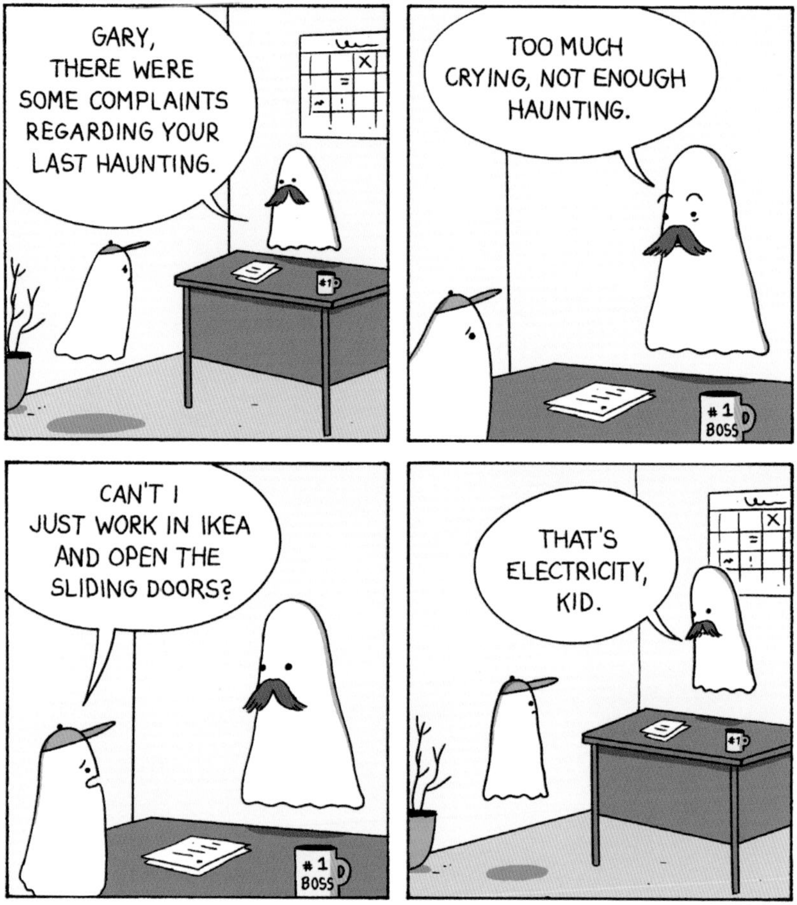
GARY, THERE WERE SOME COMPLAINTS REGARDING YOUR LAST HAUNTING.
#1
TOO MUCH CRYING, NOT ENOUGH HAUNTING.
#1 BOSS
CAN'T I JUST WORK IN IKEA AND OPEN THE SLIDING DOORS?
#1 BOSS
THAT'S ELECTRICITY, KID.
#1

FREE YOURSELF!

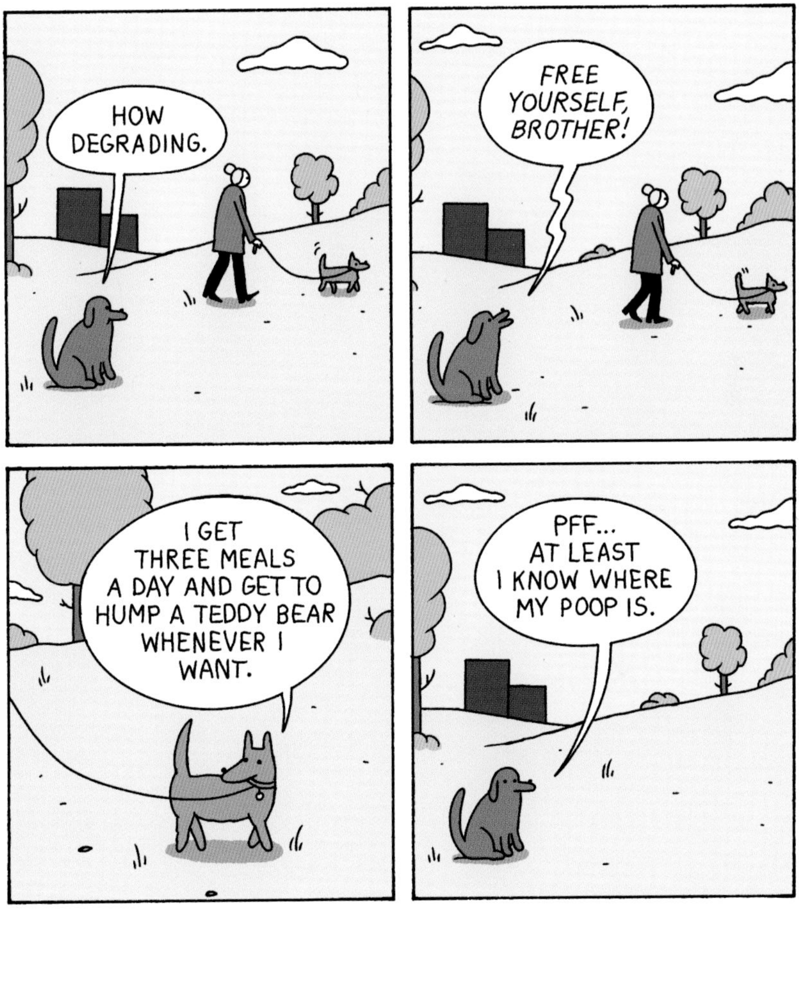

HOW DEGRADING.
FREE YOURSELF, BROTHER!
I GET THREE MEALS A DAY AND GET TO HUMP A TEDDY BEAR WHENEVER I WANT.
PFF... AT LEAST I KNOW WHERE MY POOP IS.

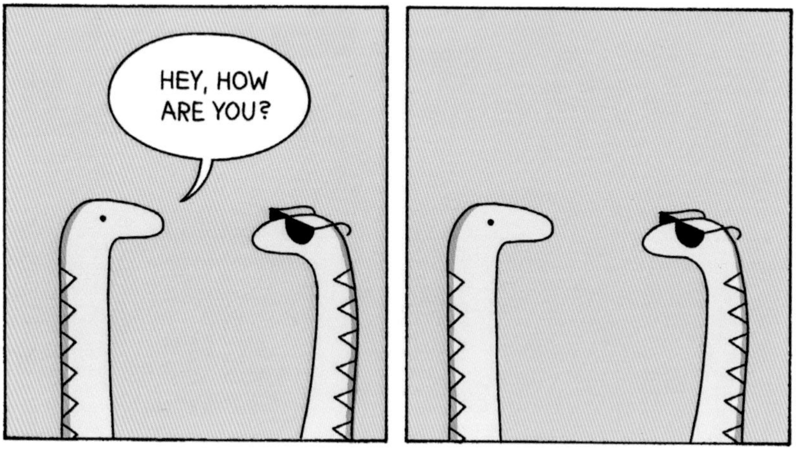
HEY, HOW ARE YOU?

BROWSER HISTORY

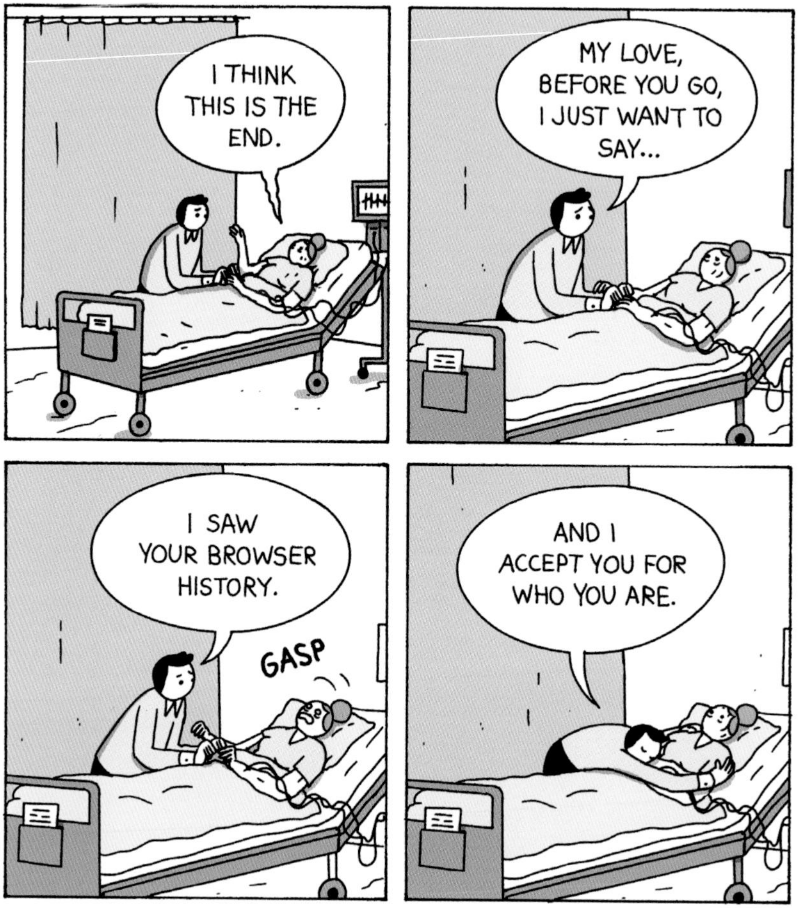
I THINK THIS IS THE END.
MY LOVE, BEFORE YOU GO, I JUST WANT TO SAY...
I SAW YOUR BROWSER HISTORY.
GASP
AND I ACCEPT YOU FOR WHO YOU ARE.

THE GREAT PRETENDER

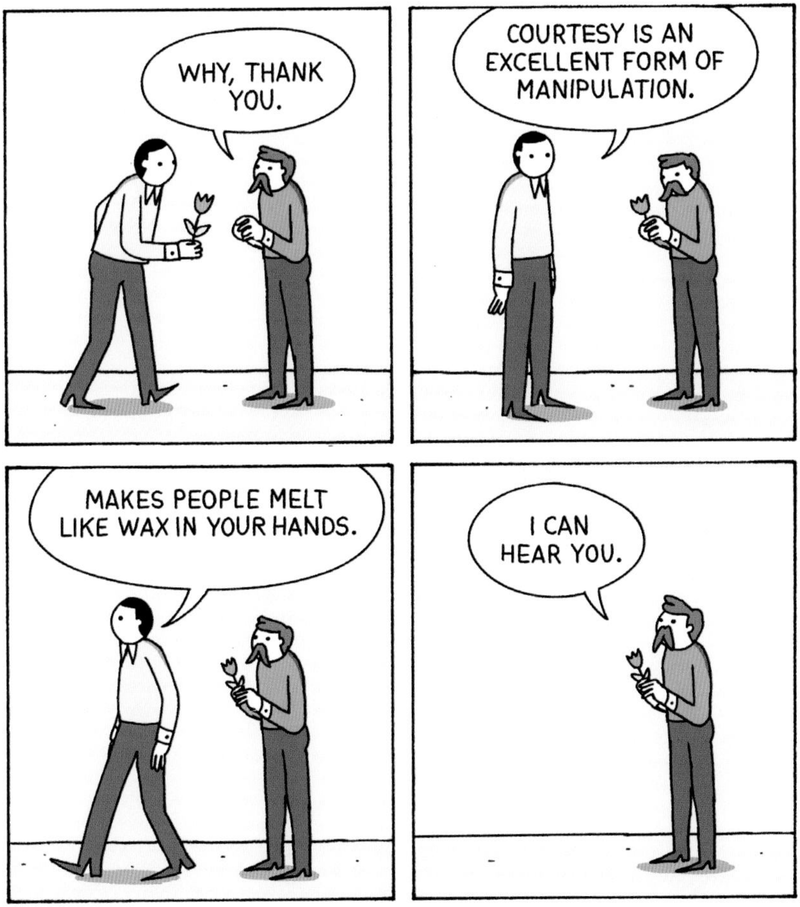

WHY, THANK YOU.
COURTESY IS AN EXCELLENT FORM OF MANIPULATION.
MAKES PEOPLE MELT LIKE WAX IN YOUR HANDS.
I CAN HEAR YOU.

TAKE ME

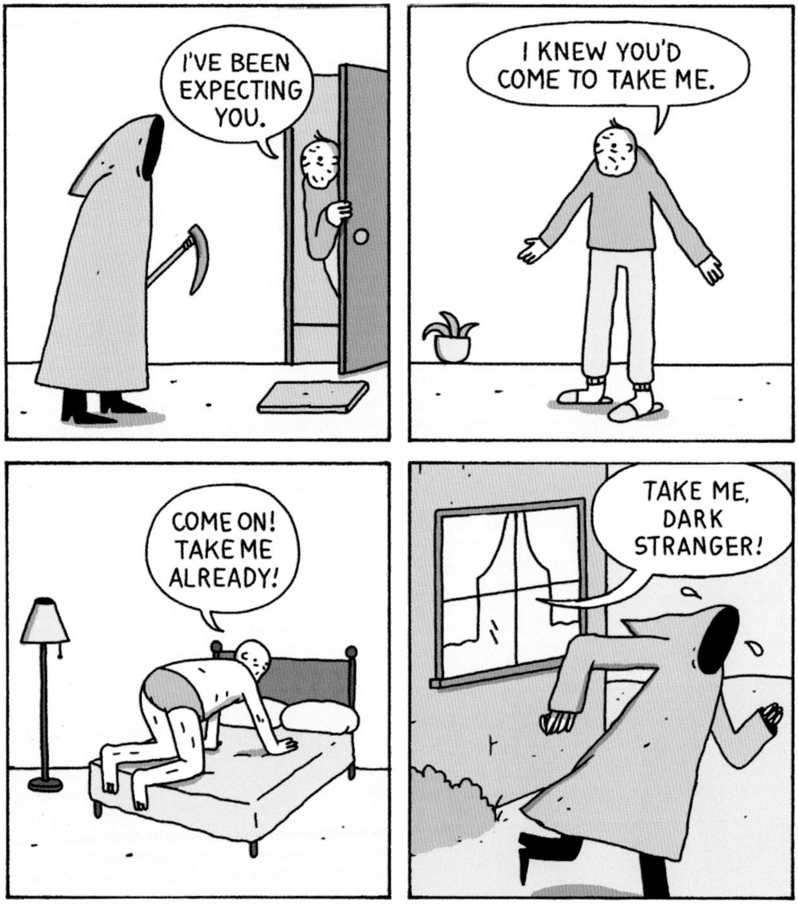
I'VE BEEN EXPECTING YOU.
I KNEW YOU'D COME TO TAKE ME.
COME ON! TAKE ME ALREADY!
TAKE ME, DARK STRANGER!

SUPERIOR

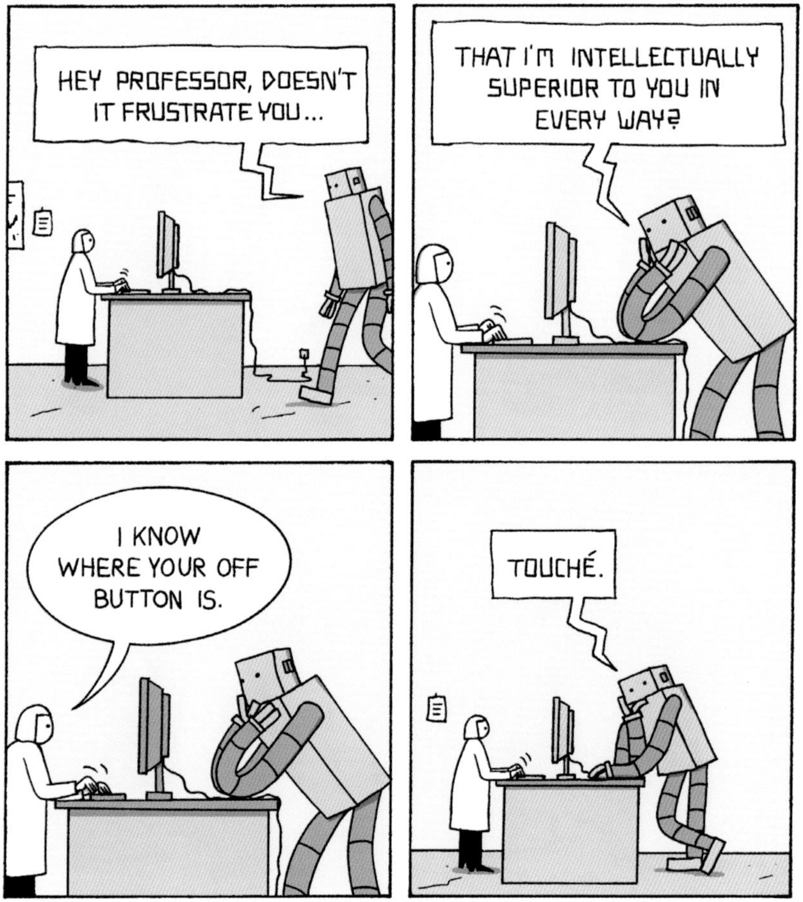

HEY PROFESSOR, DOESN'T IT FRUSTRATE YOU...
THAT I'M INTELLECTUALLY SUPERIOR TO YOU IN EVERY WAY?
I KNOW WHERE YOUR OFF BUTTON IS.
TOUCHÉ.

BIRTH OF SLUTTY WITCH

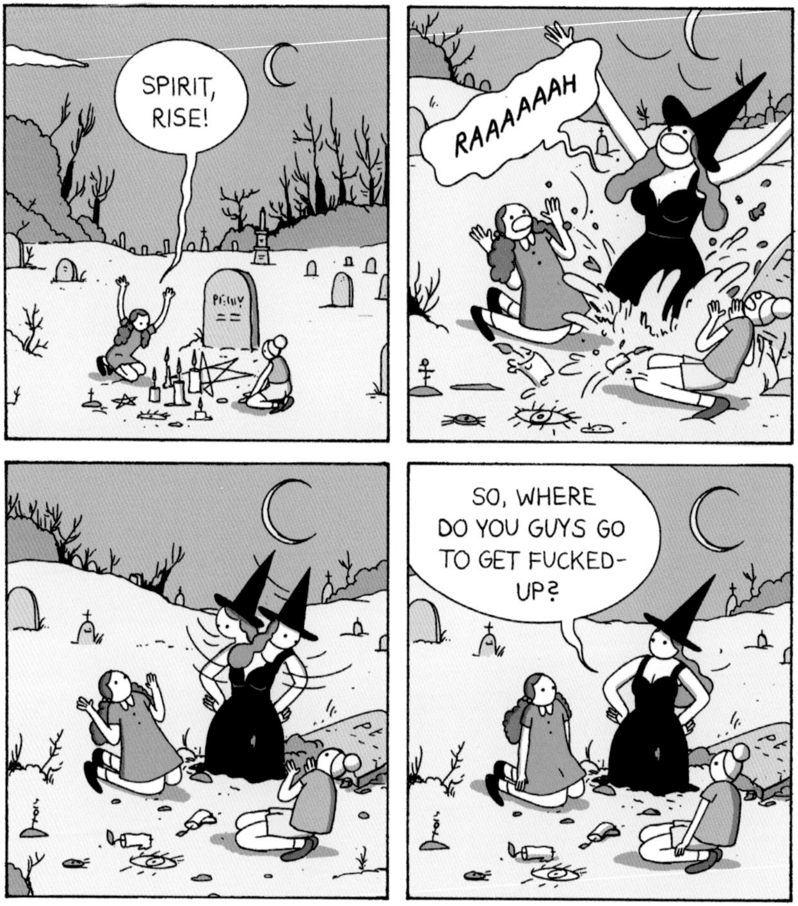

SPIRIT, RISE!
RAAAAAAH
SO, WHERE DO YOU GUYS GO TO GET FUCKED-UP?

PARANORMAL ACTIVITY

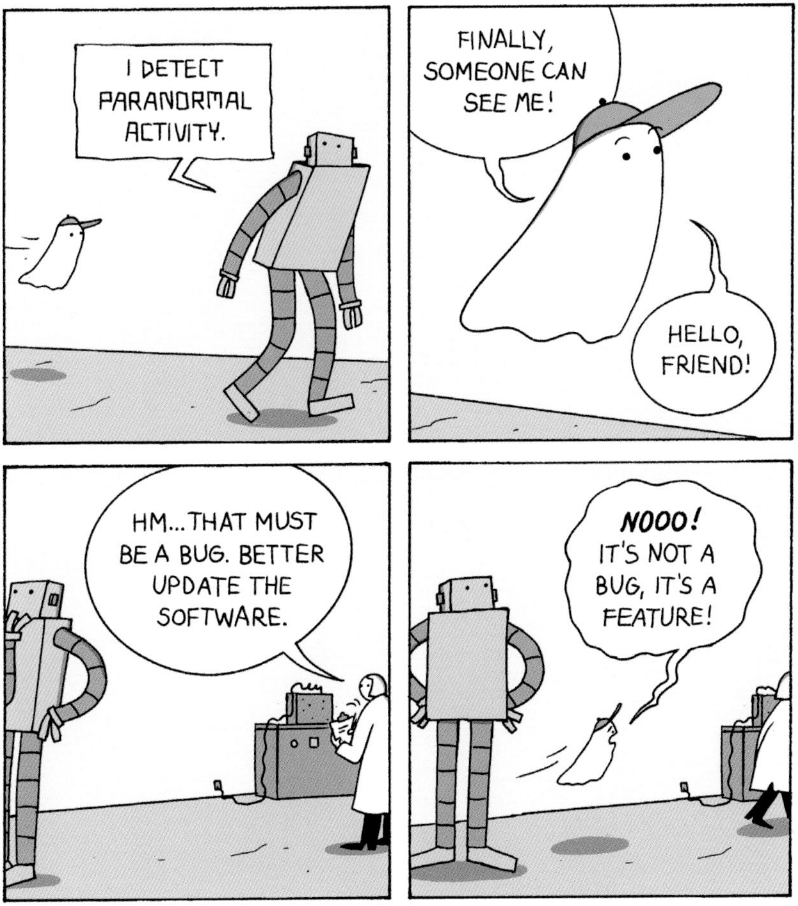
I DETECT PARANORMAL ACTIVITY.
FINALLY, SOMEONE CAN SEE ME!
HELLO, FRIEND!
HM... THAT MUST BE A BUG. BETTER UPDATE THE SOFTWARE.
NOOO! IT'S NOT A BUG, IT'S A FEATURE!

B.A.

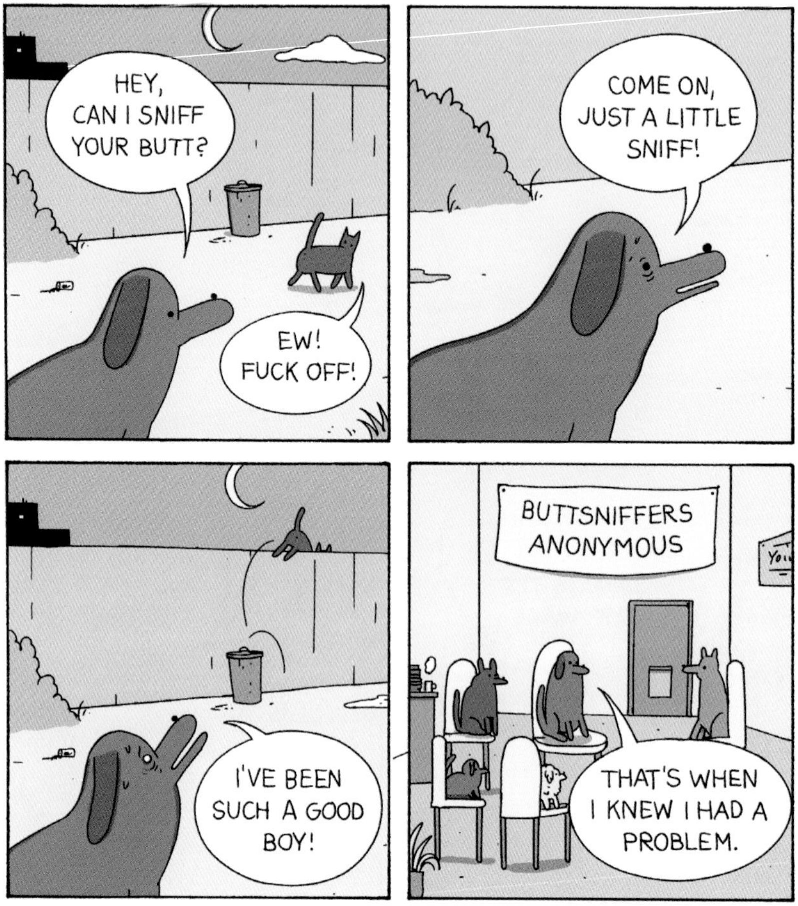
HEY, CAN I SNIFF YOUR BUTT?
EW! FUCK OFF!
COME ON, JUST A LITTLE SNIFF!
I'VE BEEN SUCH A GOOD BOY!
BUTTSNIFFERS ANONYMOUS
THAT'S WHEN I KNEW I HAD A PROBLEM.

SLUTTY WITCH

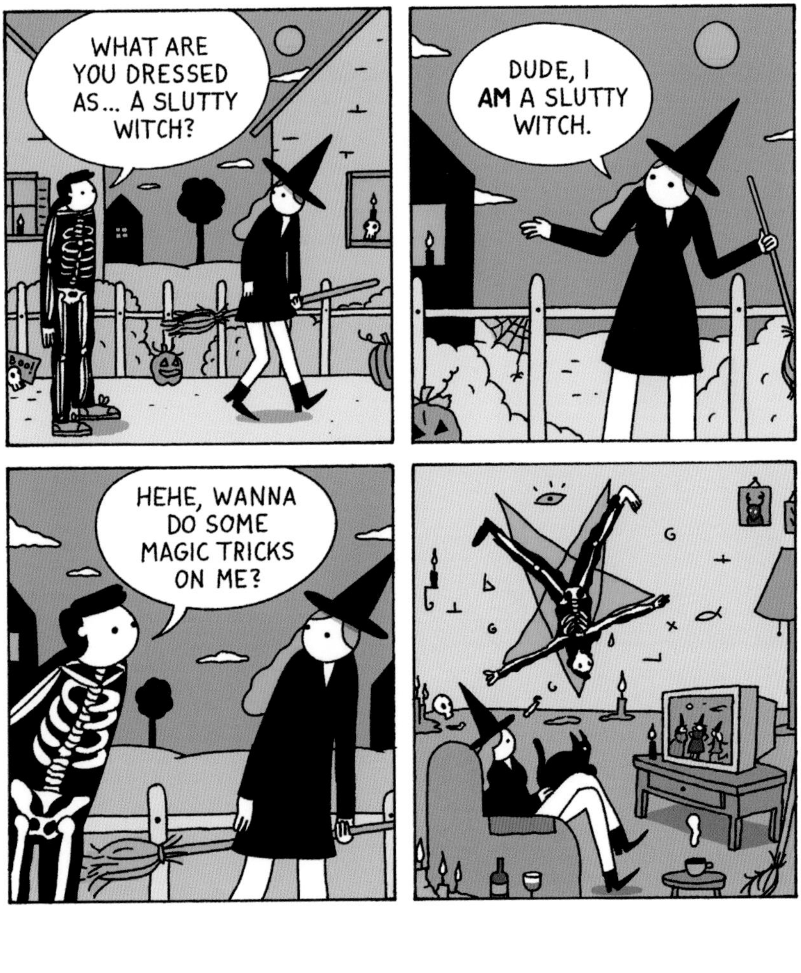
WHAT ARE YOU DRESSED AS... A SLUTTY WITCH?
DUDE, I **AM** A SLUTTY WITCH.
HEHE, WANNA DO SOME MAGIC TRICKS ON ME?
BOO!

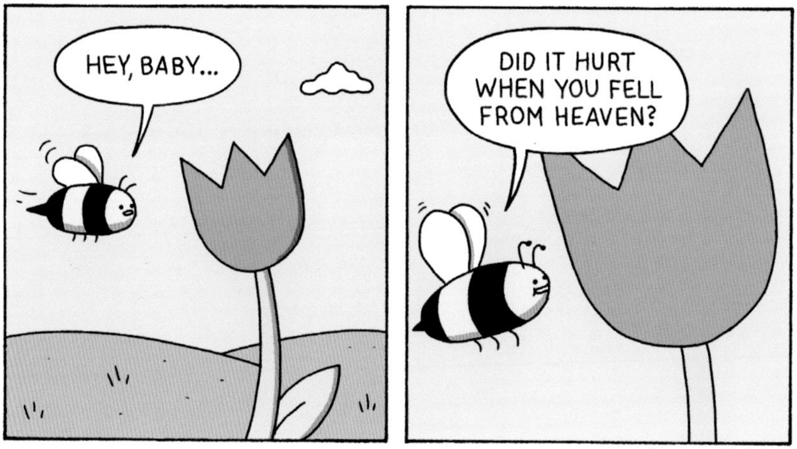
HEY, BABY...
DID IT HURT WHEN YOU FELL FROM HEAVEN?

EXHAUSTED

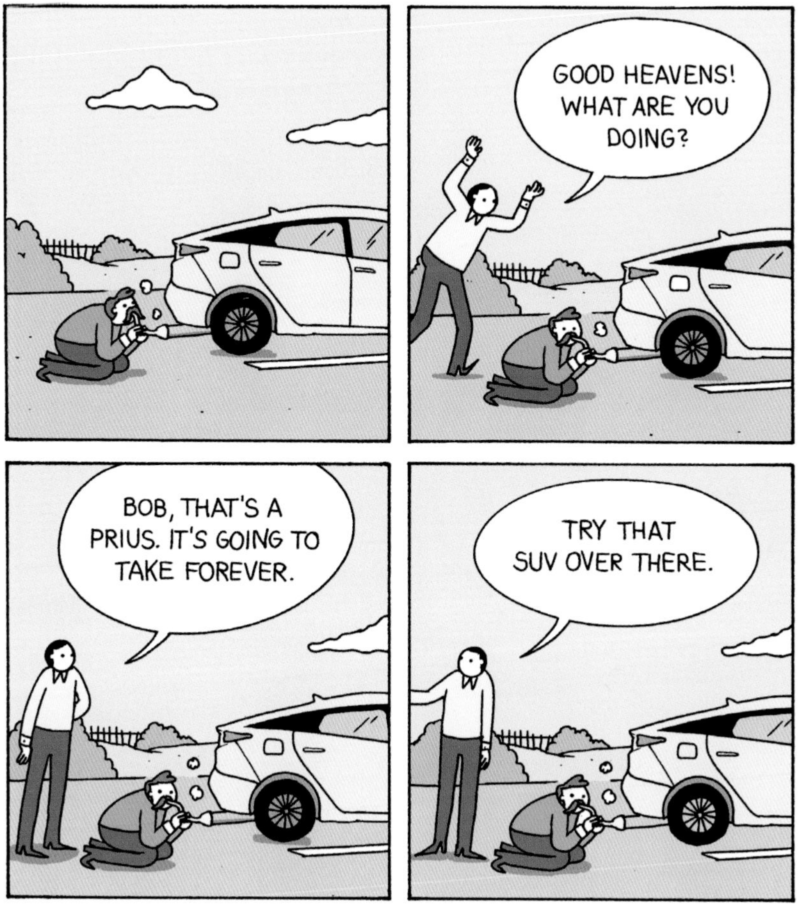
GOOD HEAVENS! WHAT ARE YOU DOING?
BOB, THAT'S A PRIUS. IT'S GOING TO TAKE FOREVER.
TRY THAT SUV OVER THERE.

NEAR-DEATH EXPERIENCE

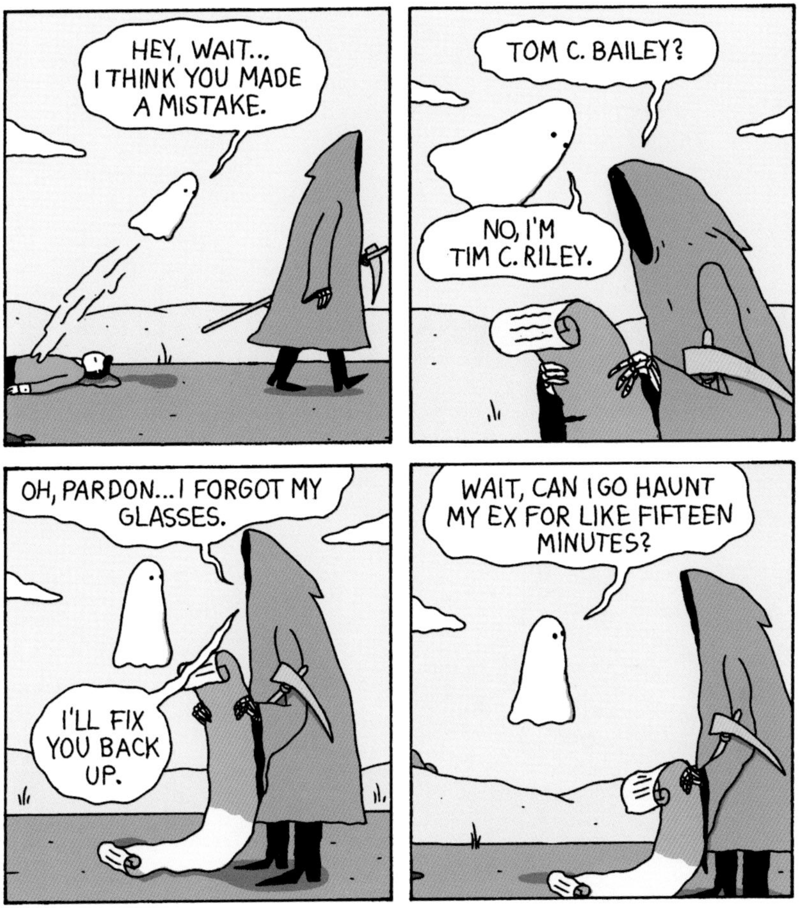

HEY, WAIT... I THINK YOU MADE A MISTAKE.
TOM C. BAILEY?
NO, I'M TIM C. RILEY.
OH, PARDON... I FORGOT MY GLASSES.
I'LL FIX YOU BACK UP.
WAIT, CAN I GO HAUNT MY EX FOR LIKE FIFTEEN MINUTES?

A POEM

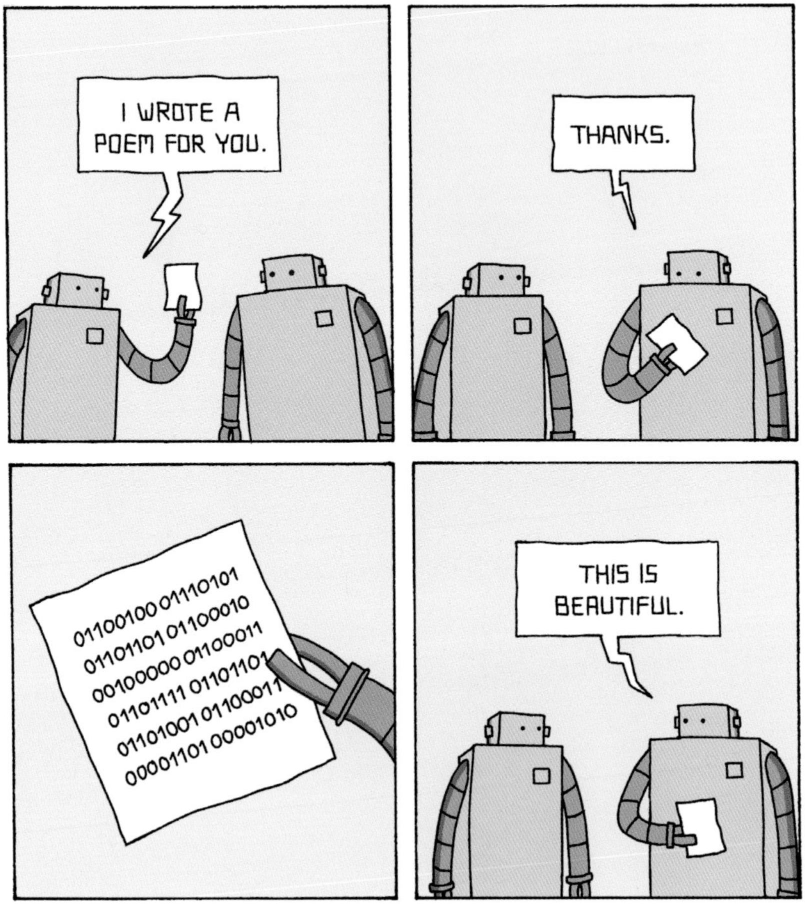

I WROTE A POEM FOR YOU.
THANKS.
01100100 01110101
01101101 01100010
00100000 01100011
01101111 01101101
01101001 01100011
00001101 00001010
THIS IS BEAUTIFUL.

ANOTHER SKULL

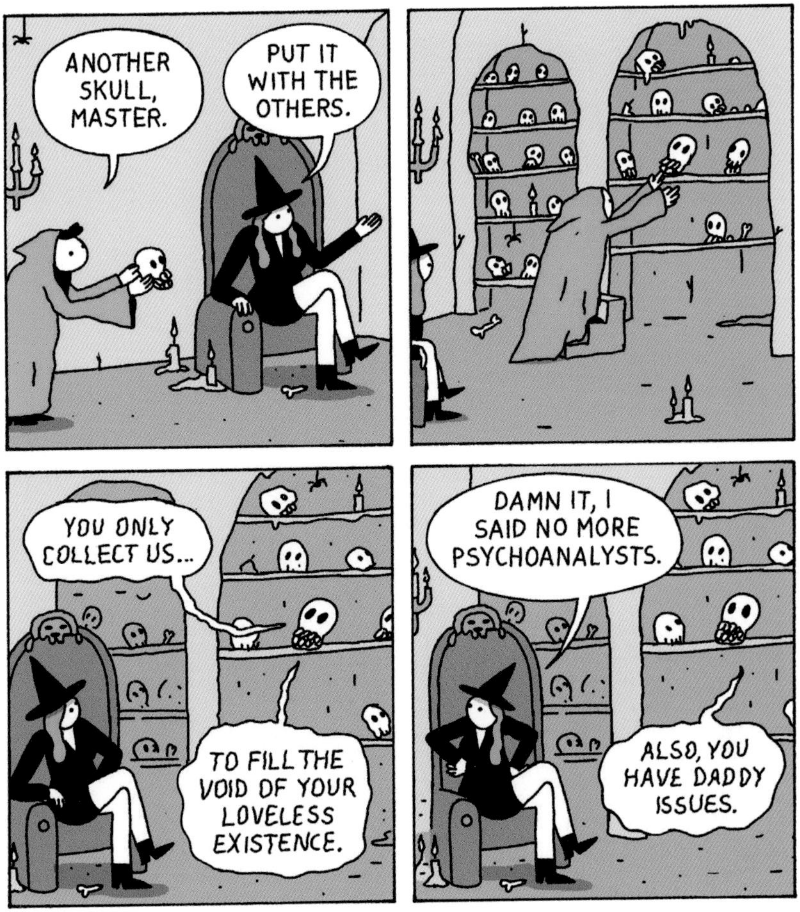
ANOTHER SKULL, MASTER.
PUT IT WITH THE OTHERS.
YOU ONLY COLLECT US...
TO FILL THE VOID OF YOUR LOVELESS EXISTENCE.
DAMN IT, I SAID NO MORE PSYCHOANALYSTS.
ALSO, YOU HAVE DADDY ISSUES.

REALLY SCARY COSTUME

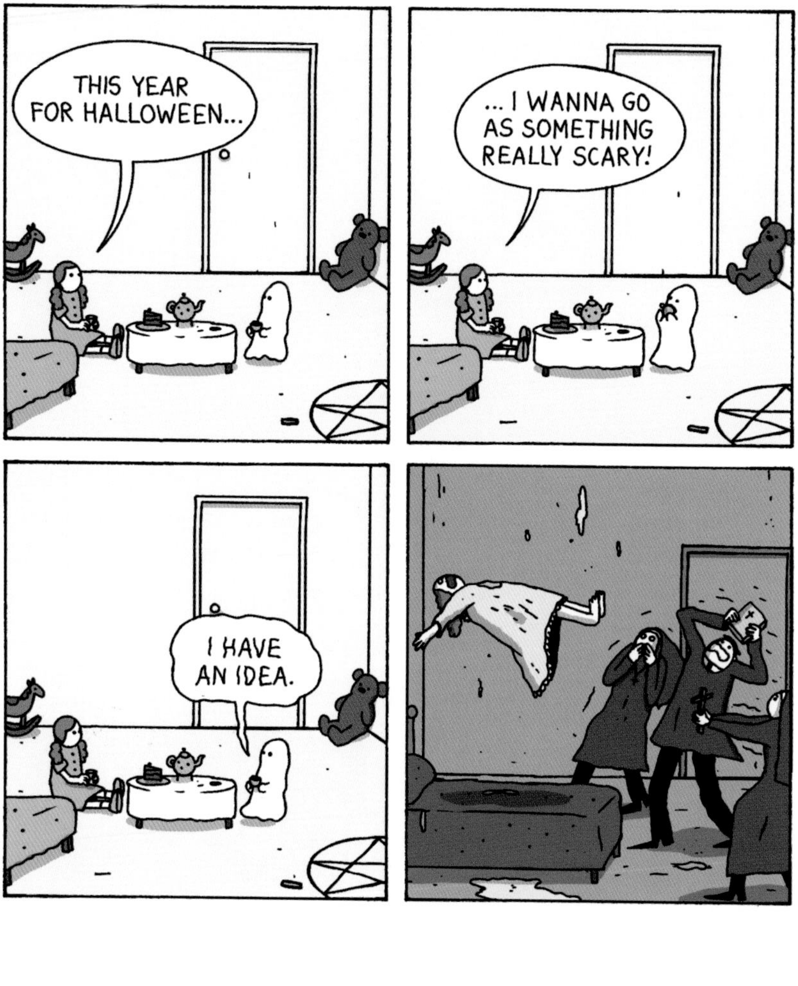

THIS YEAR FOR HALLOWEEN...
... I WANNA GO AS SOMETHING REALLY SCARY!
I HAVE AN IDEA.

MAN'S BEST FRIEND

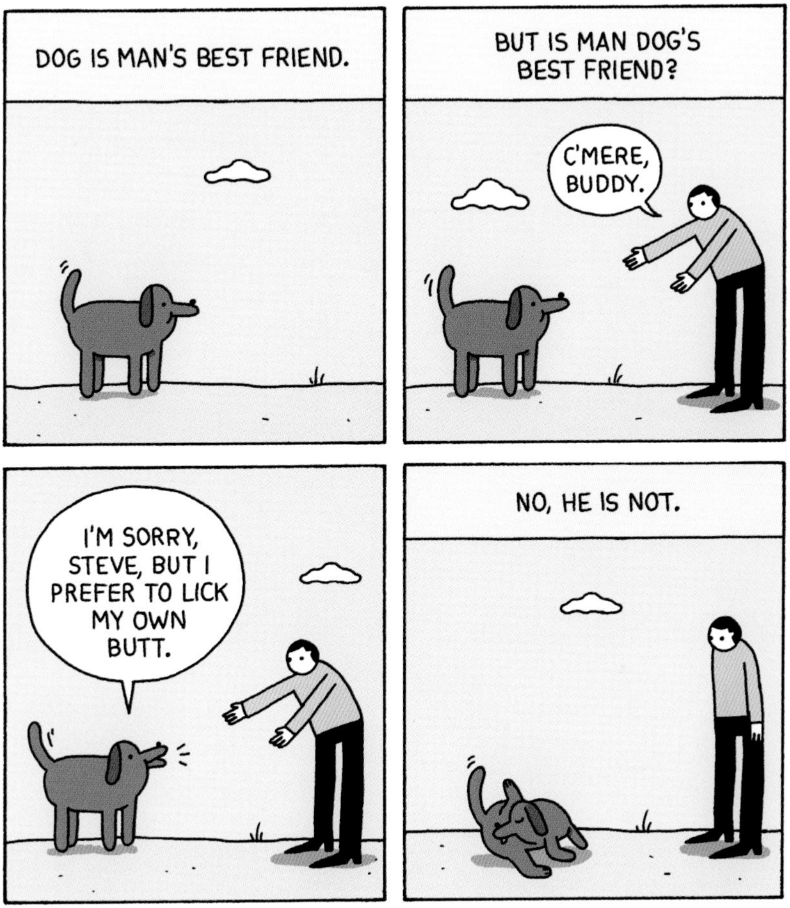
DOG IS MAN'S BEST FRIEND.
BUT IS MAN DOG'S BEST FRIEND?
C'MERE, BUDDY.
I'M SORRY, STEVE, BUT I PREFER TO LICK MY OWN BUTT.
NO, HE IS NOT.

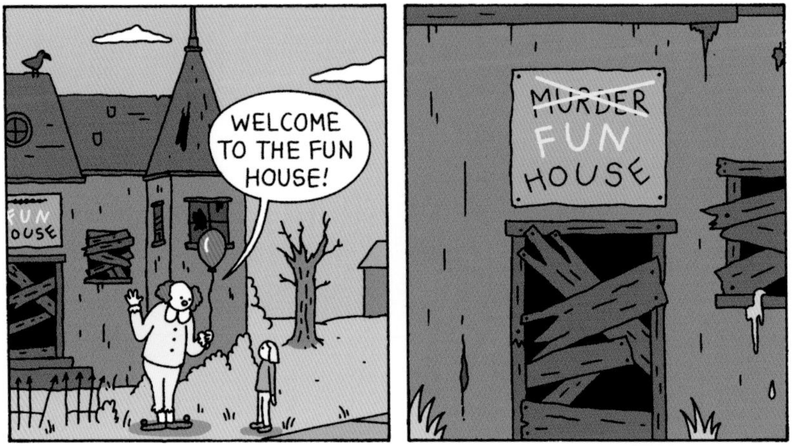
WELCOME TO THE FUN HOUSE!
MURDER
FUN
HOUSE

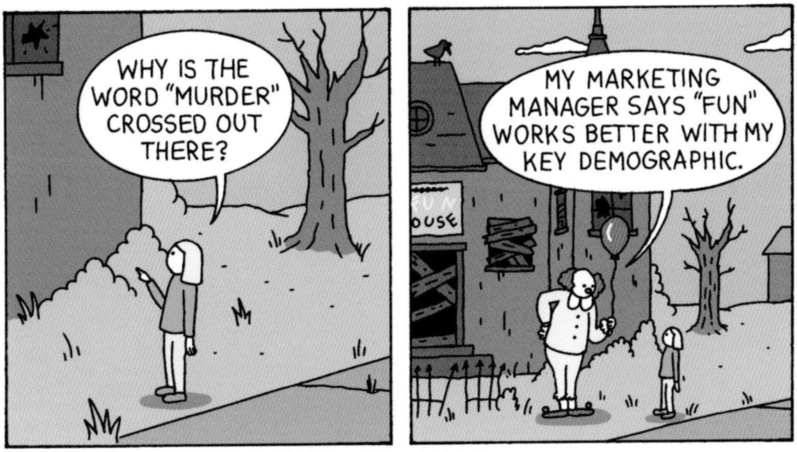
WHY IS THE WORD "MURDER" CROSSED OUT THERE?
MY MARKETING MANAGER SAYS "FUN" WORKS BETTER WITH MY KEY DEMOGRAPHIC.

WITCH-HUMPER

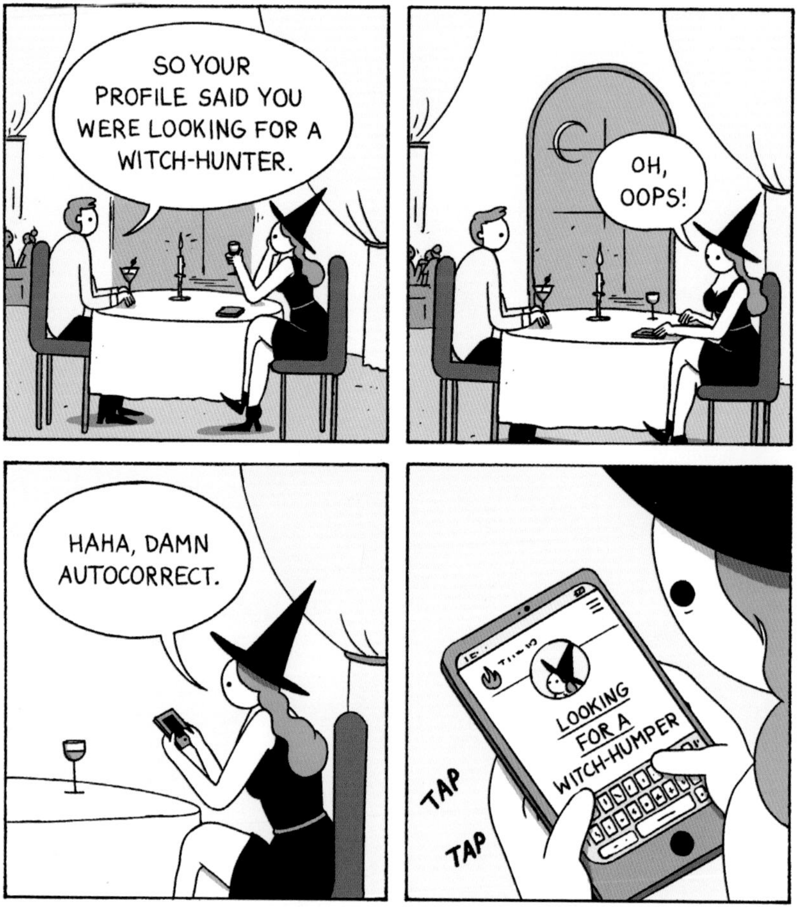
SO YOUR PROFILE SAID YOU WERE LOOKING FOR A WITCH-HUNTER.
OH, OOPS!
HAHA, DAMN AUTOCORRECT.
LOOKING FOR A WITCH-HUMPER
TAP
TAP

JUST A FEELING

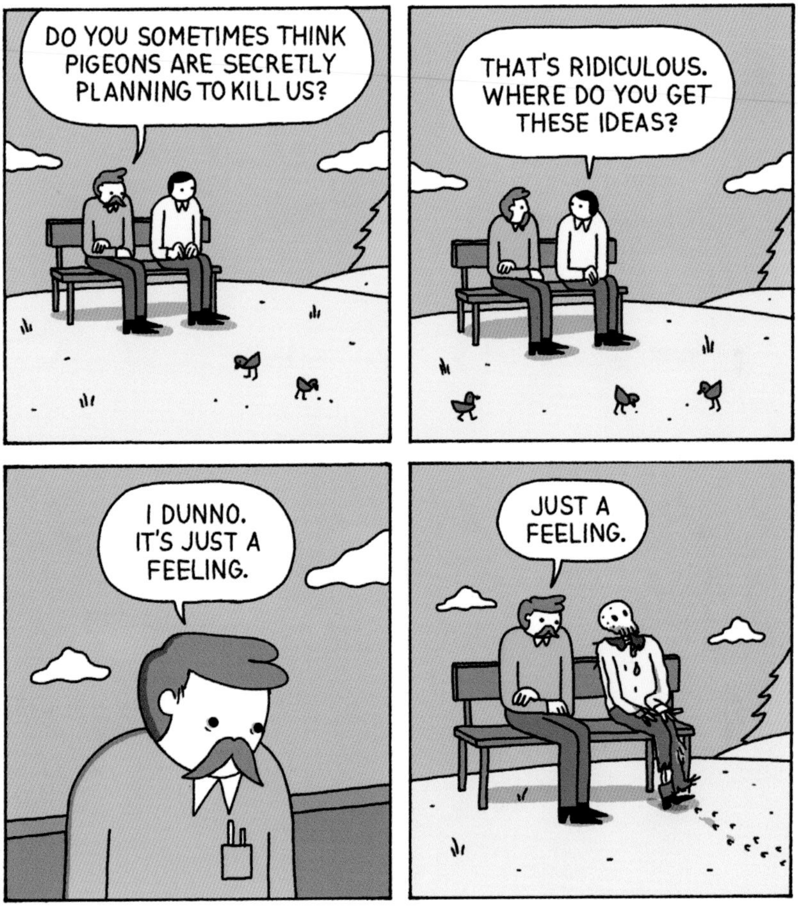

DO YOU SOMETIMES THINK PIGEONS ARE SECRETLY PLANNING TO KILL US?
THAT'S RIDICULOUS. WHERE DO YOU GET THESE IDEAS?
I DUNNO. IT'S JUST A FEELING.
JUST A FEELING.

WHERE THE CORPSES GO

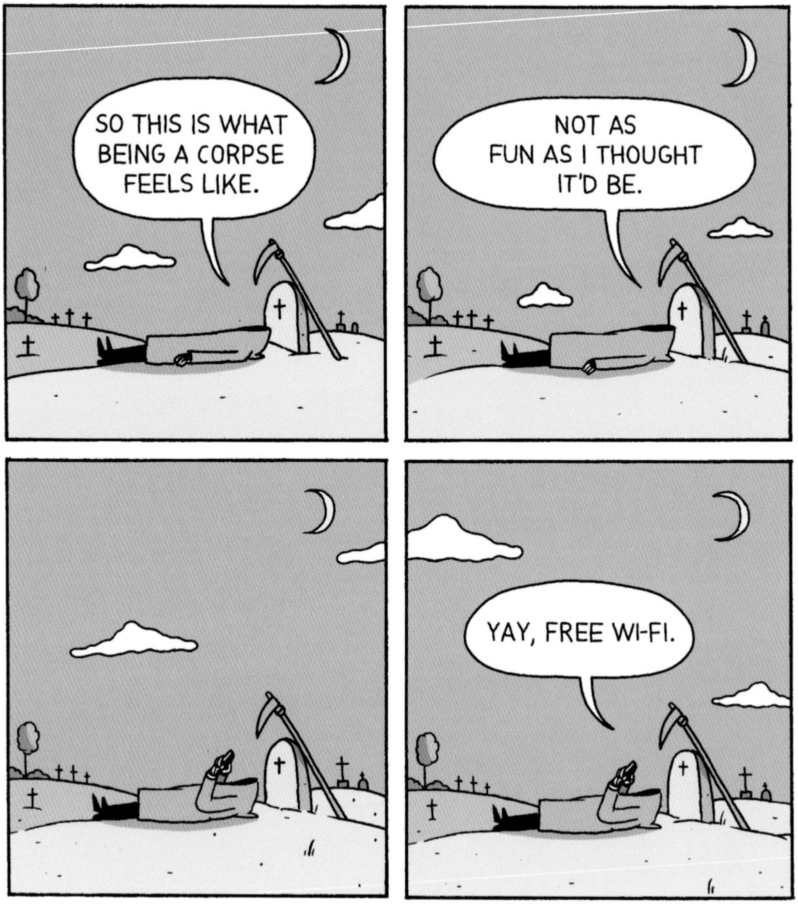
SO THIS IS WHAT BEING A CORPSE FEELS LIKE.
NOT AS FUN AS I THOUGHT IT'D BE.
YAY, FREE WI-FI.

MESSED UP

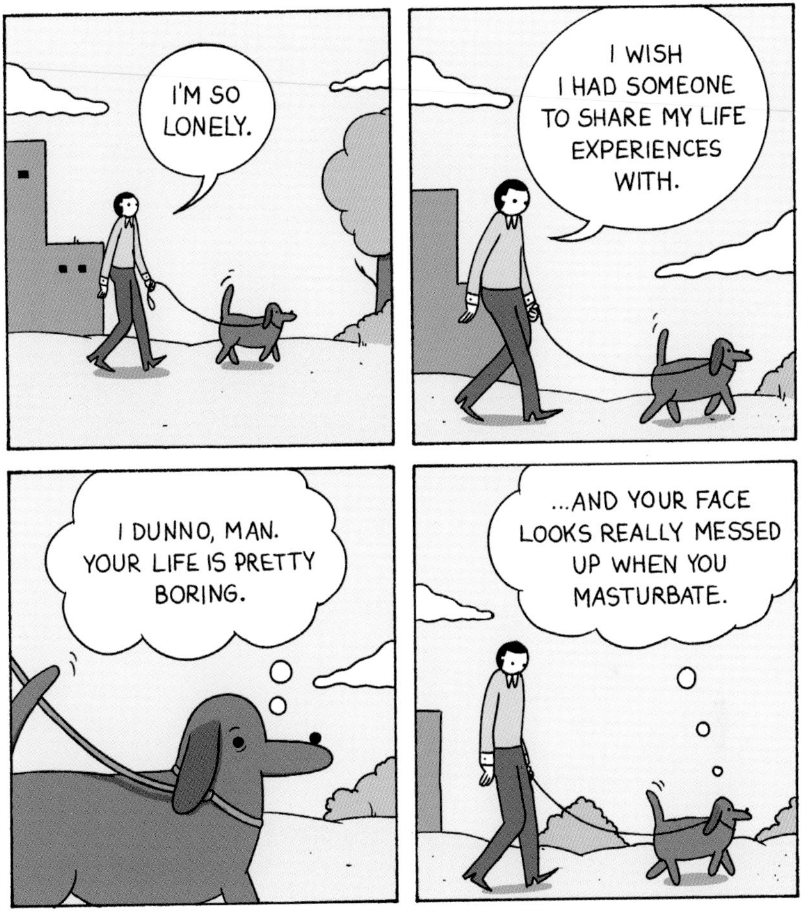

I'M SO LONELY.
I WISH I HAD SOMEONE TO SHARE MY LIFE EXPERIENCES WITH.
I DUNNO, MAN. YOUR LIFE IS PRETTY BORING.
...AND YOUR FACE LOOKS REALLY MESSED UP WHEN YOU MASTURBATE.

ON THE EDGE

GARY DECIDED TO LIVE ON THE EDGE.
HE COULD DO THAT, AS HE WAS A GHOST.
I CAN SEE YOUR UNDERPANTS!
GHOSTS CAN GET EMBARRASSED, TOO.

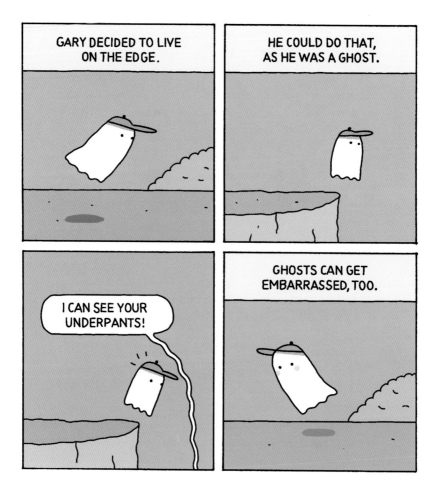

GOOD STUFF

PSST, PAL, LOOKS LIKE YOU COULD USE...
A HUG.
THAT'LL BE 20 BUCKS.

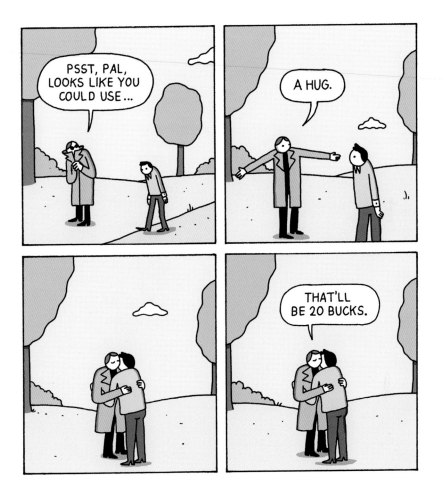

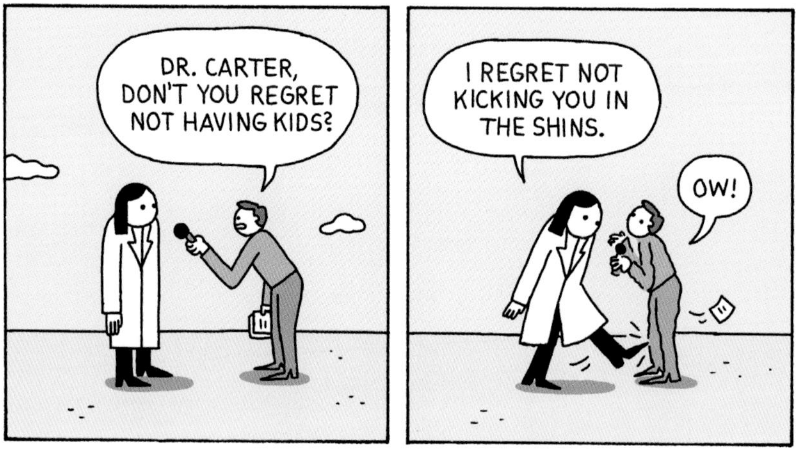
DR. CARTER, DON'T YOU REGRET NOT HAVING KIDS?
I REGRET NOT KICKING YOU IN THE SHINS.
OW!

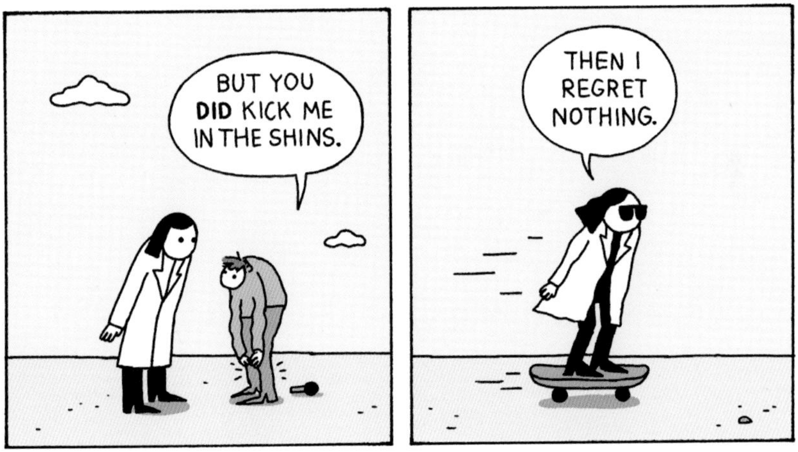
BUT YOU **DID** KICK ME IN THE SHINS.
THEN I REGRET NOTHING.

DATING LIFE

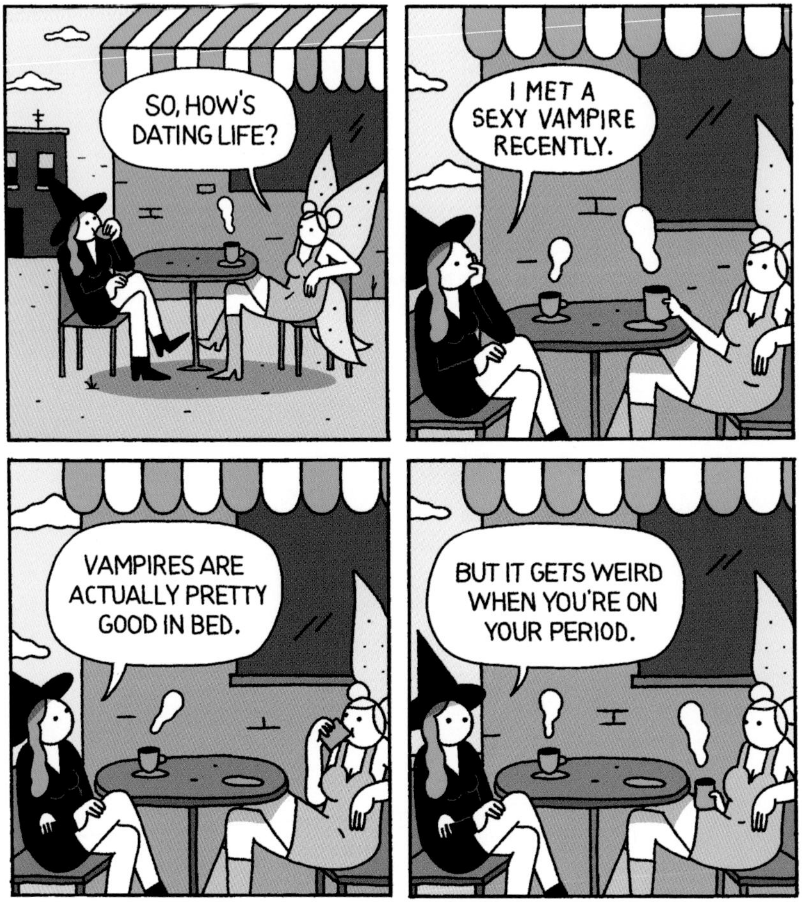

SO, HOW'S DATING LIFE?
I MET A SEXY VAMPIRE RECENTLY.
VAMPIRES ARE ACTUALLY PRETTY GOOD IN BED.
BUT IT GETS WEIRD WHEN YOU'RE ON YOUR PERIOD.

TIME IS RELATIVE

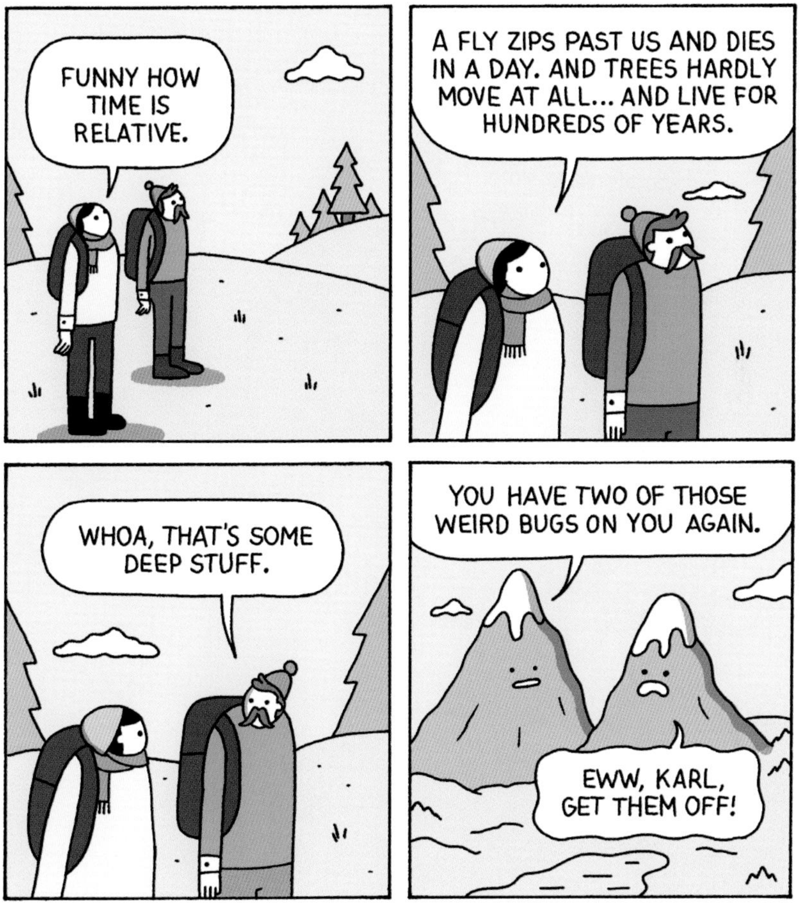
FUNNY HOW TIME IS RELATIVE.
A FLY ZIPS PAST US AND DIES IN A DAY. AND TREES HARDLY MOVE AT ALL... AND LIVE FOR HUNDREDS OF YEARS.
WHOA, THAT'S SOME DEEP STUFF.
YOU HAVE TWO OF THOSE WEIRD BUGS ON YOU AGAIN.
EWW, KARL, GET THEM OFF!

I LOVE YOU, SLUTTY WITCH

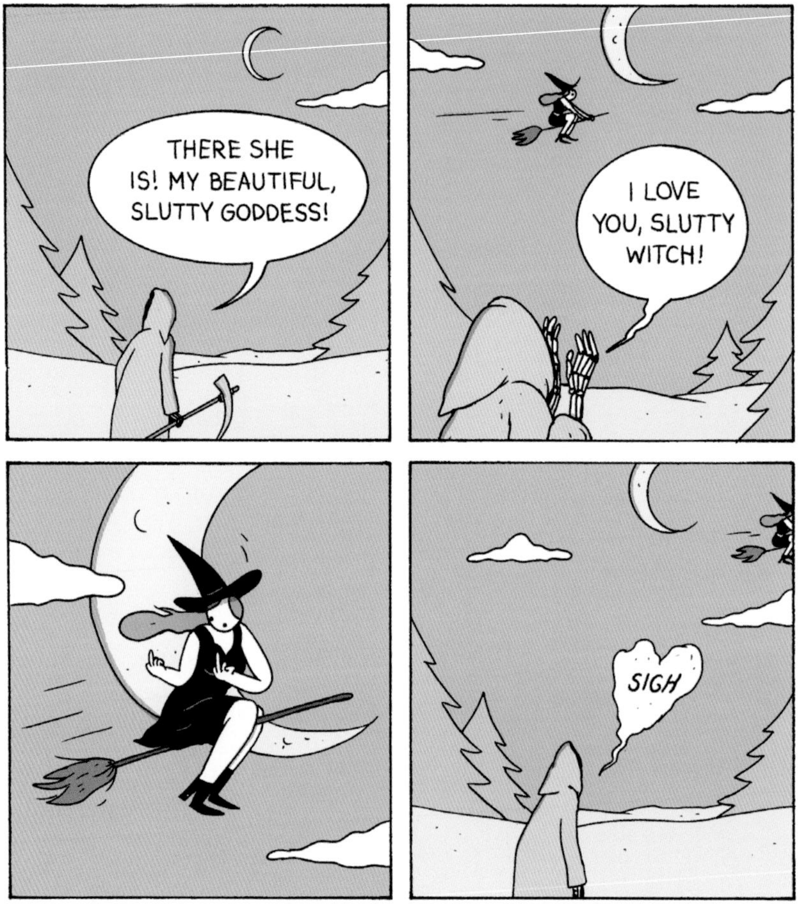
THERE SHE IS! MY BEAUTIFUL, SLUTTY GODDESS!
I LOVE YOU, SLUTTY WITCH!
SIGH

ATTRACTION

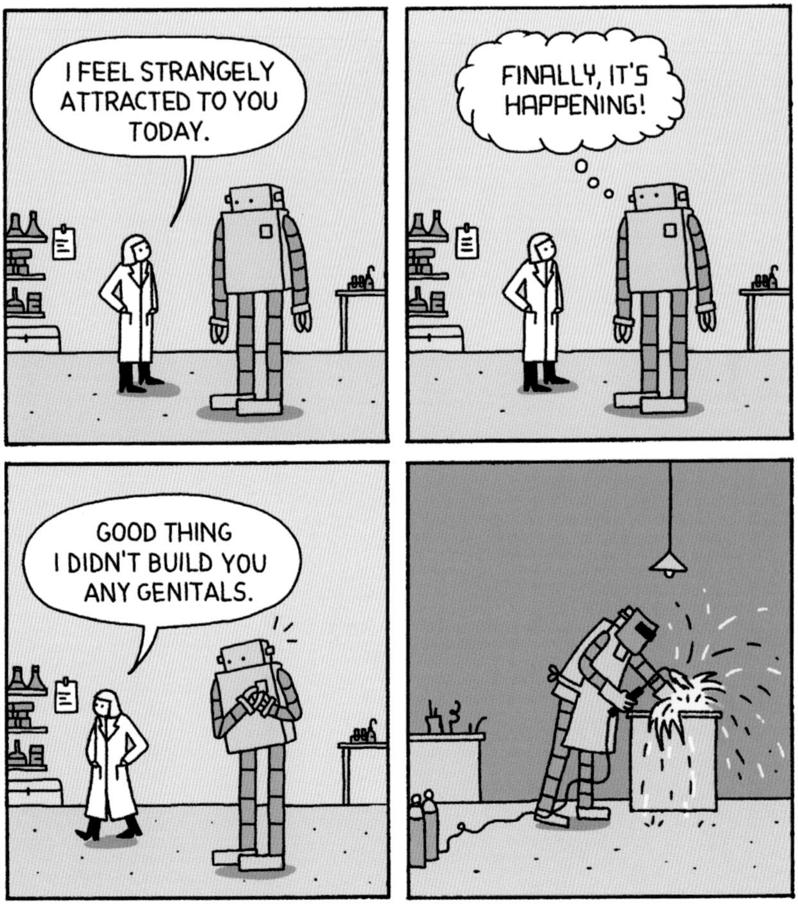
I FEEL STRANGELY ATTRACTED TO YOU TODAY.
FINALLY, IT'S HAPPENING!
GOOD THING I DIDN'T BUILD YOU ANY GENITALS.

MY SIX-YEAR-OLD

HA...
MY SIX-YEAR-OLD COULD'VE DRAWN THAT.
SIR, YOUR SIX-YEAR-OLD DID DRAW THAT.
GET THAT BITCH OUTTA HERE.

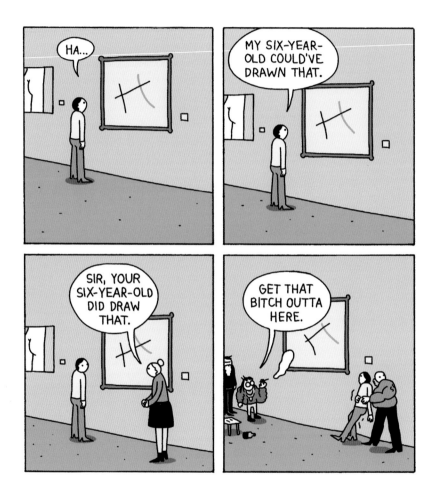

BEST FRIENDS

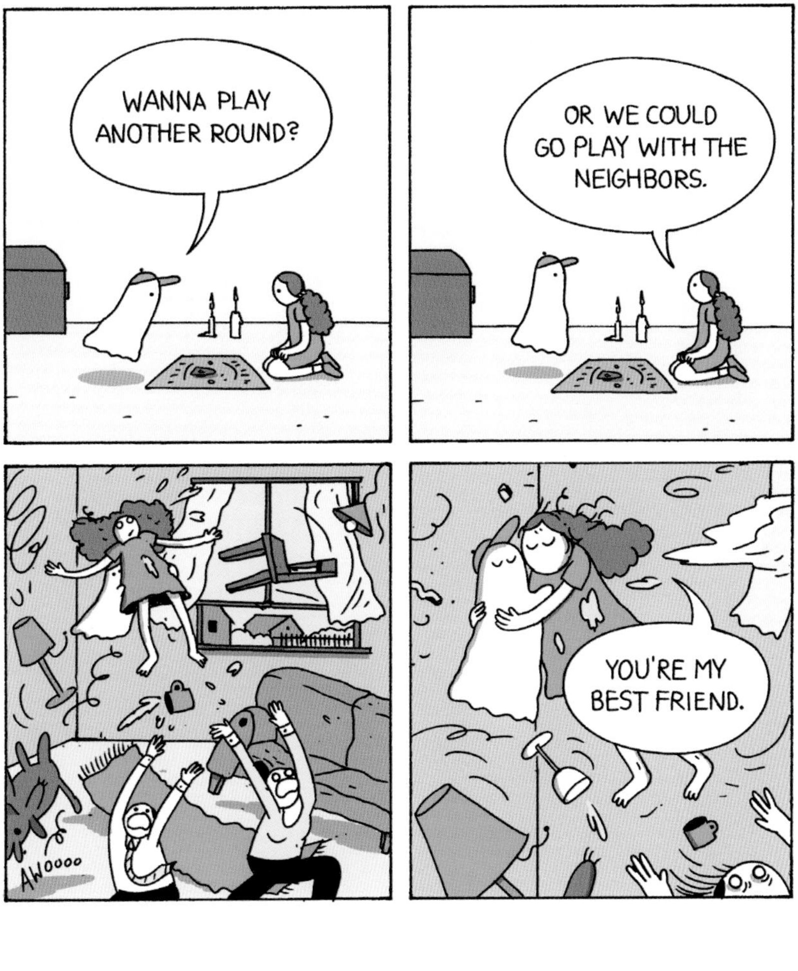
WANNA PLAY ANOTHER ROUND?
OR WE COULD GO PLAY WITH THE NEIGHBORS.
AWOOOO
YOU'RE MY BEST FRIEND.

GOOD BOY

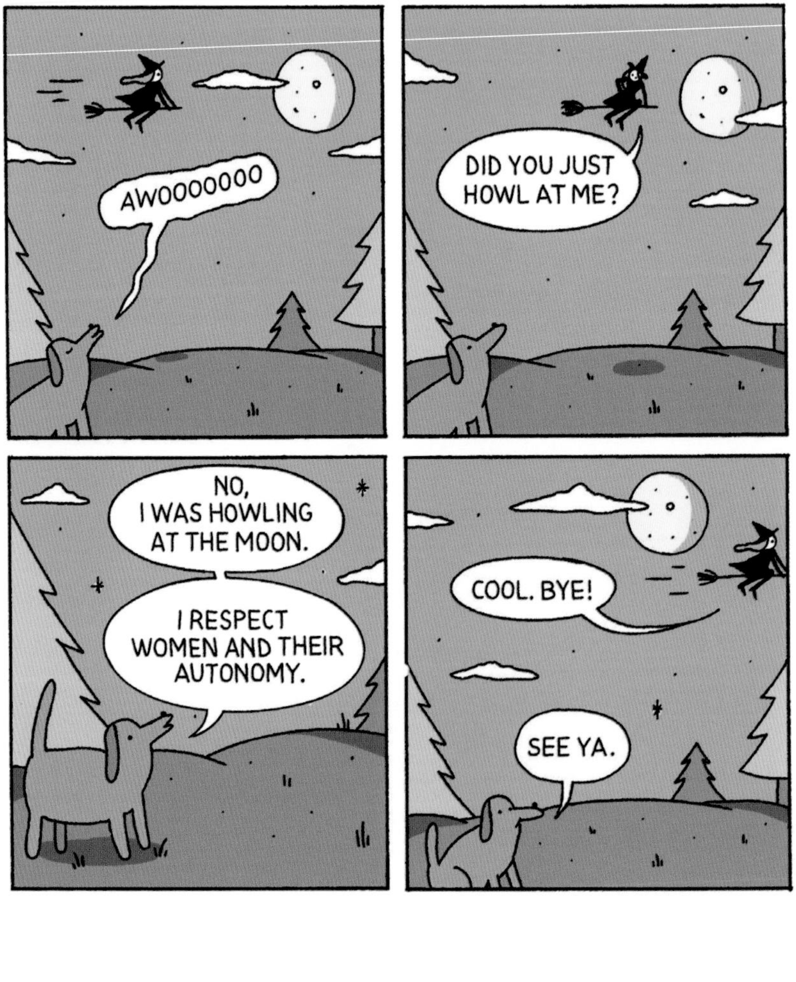
AWOOOOOOO
DID YOU JUST HOWL AT ME?
NO, I WAS HOWLING AT THE MOON.
I RESPECT WOMEN AND THEIR AUTONOMY.
COOL. BYE!
SEE YA.

THE SEEDLESS WATERMELON

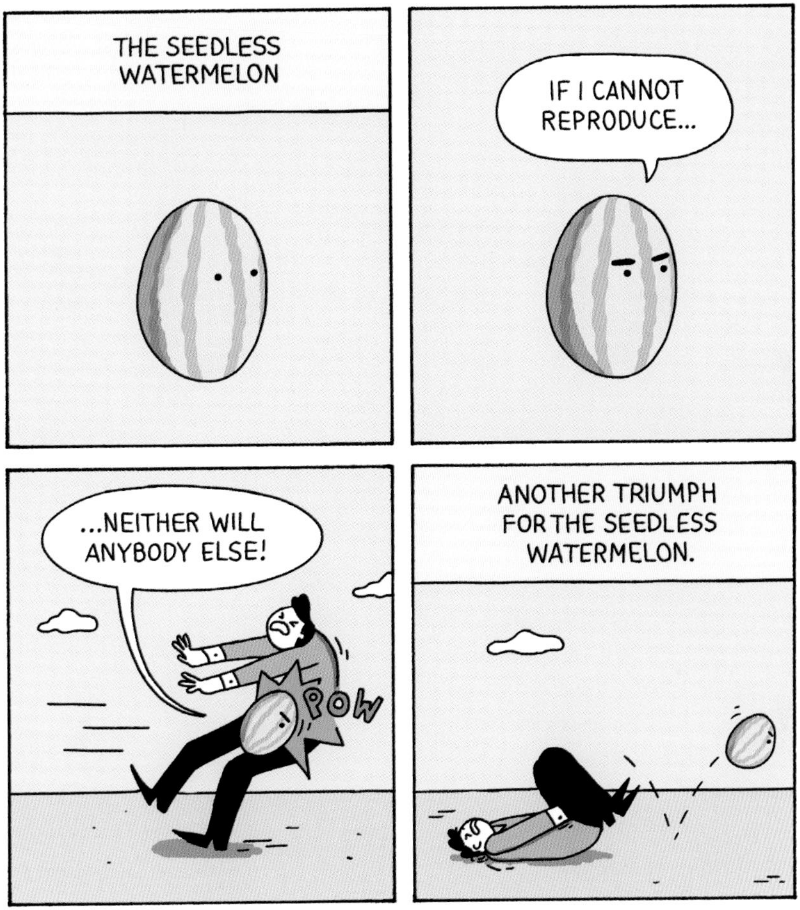

THE SEEDLESS WATERMELON
IF I CANNOT REPRODUCE...
...NEITHER WILL ANYBODY ELSE!
POW
ANOTHER TRIUMPH FOR THE SEEDLESS WATERMELON.

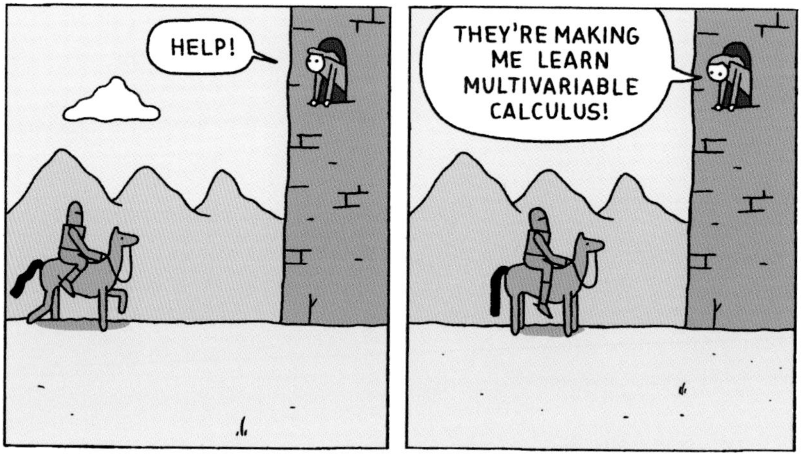
HELP!
THEY'RE MAKING ME LEARN MULTIVARIABLE CALCULUS!

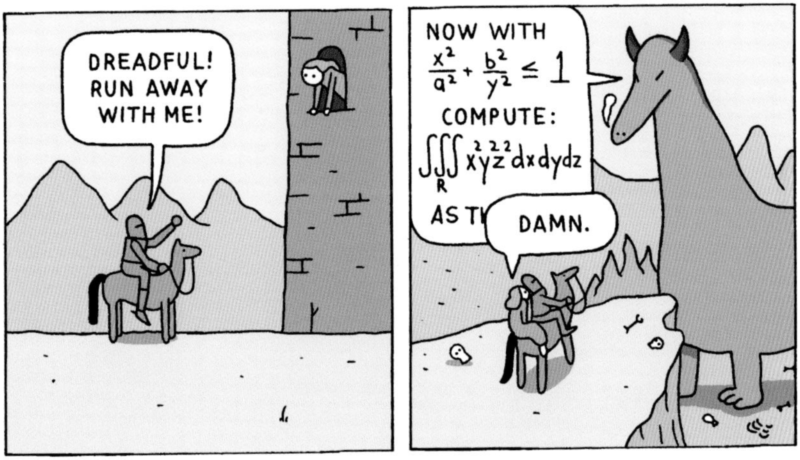
DREADFUL! RUN AWAY WITH ME!
NOW WITH $\frac{x^2}{a^2} + \frac{b^2}{y^2} \leq 1$ COMPUTE: $\iiint_R x^2y^2z^2\,dx\,dy\,dz$ AS T
DAMN.

DINNER'S READY

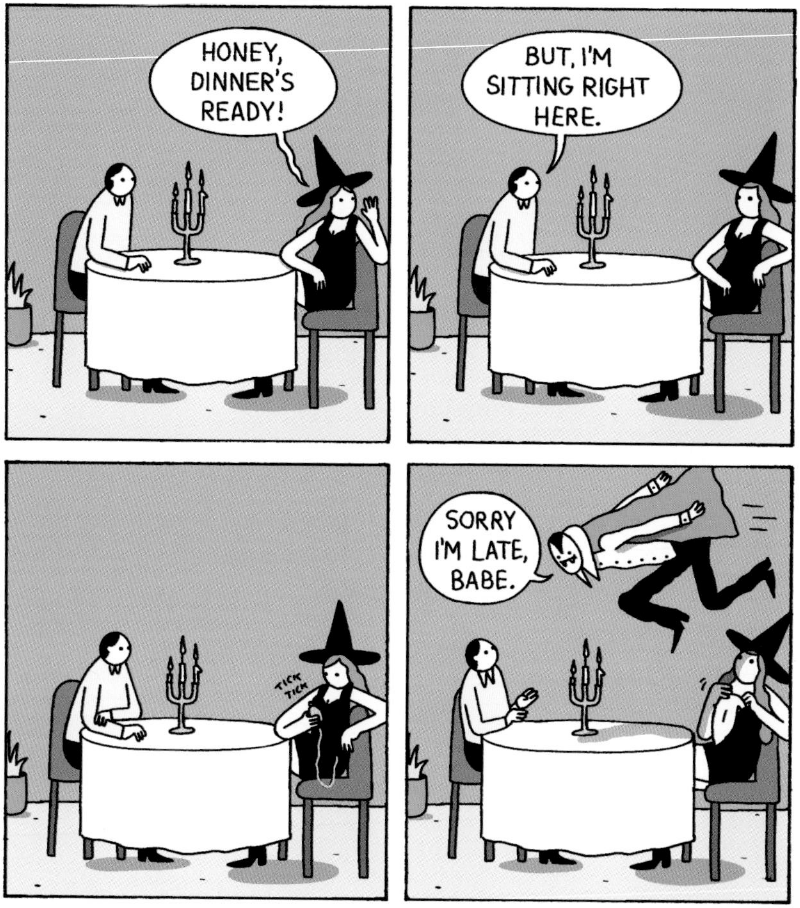
HONEY, DINNER'S READY!
BUT, I'M SITTING RIGHT HERE.
TICK TICK
SORRY I'M LATE, BABE.

DOCTOR DEATH

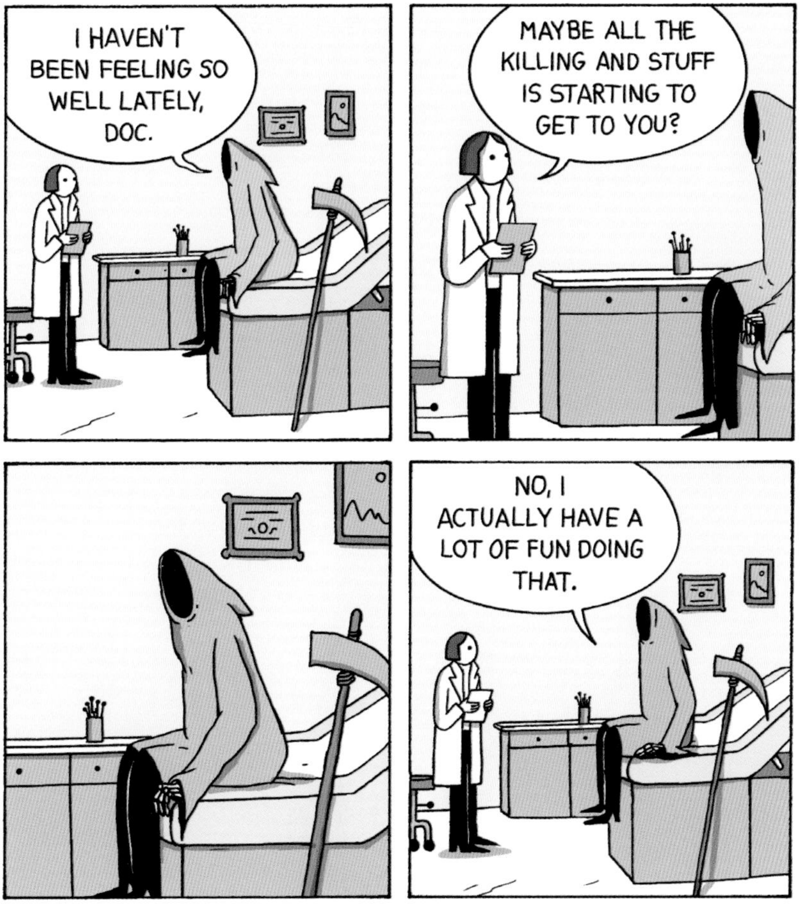
I HAVEN'T BEEN FEELING SO WELL LATELY, DOC.
MAYBE ALL THE KILLING AND STUFF IS STARTING TO GET TO YOU?
NO, I ACTUALLY HAVE A LOT OF FUN DOING THAT.

LIPSTICK

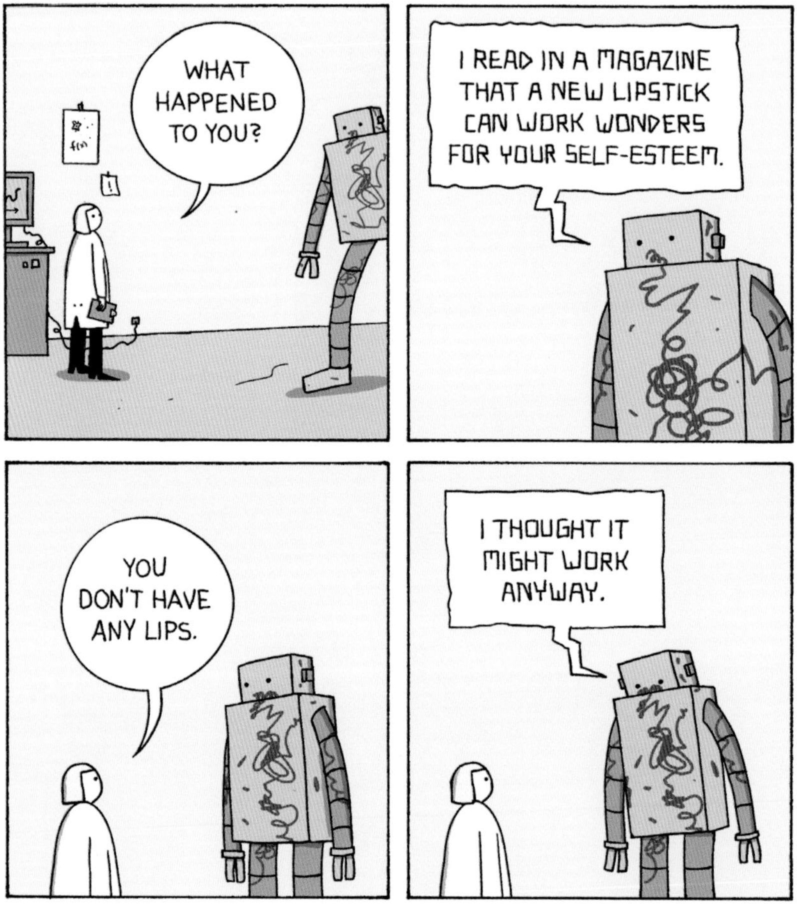
WHAT HAPPENED TO YOU?
I READ IN A MAGAZINE THAT A NEW LIPSTICK CAN WORK WONDERS FOR YOUR SELF-ESTEEM.
YOU DON'T HAVE ANY LIPS.
I THOUGHT IT MIGHT WORK ANYWAY.

LAUNDRY

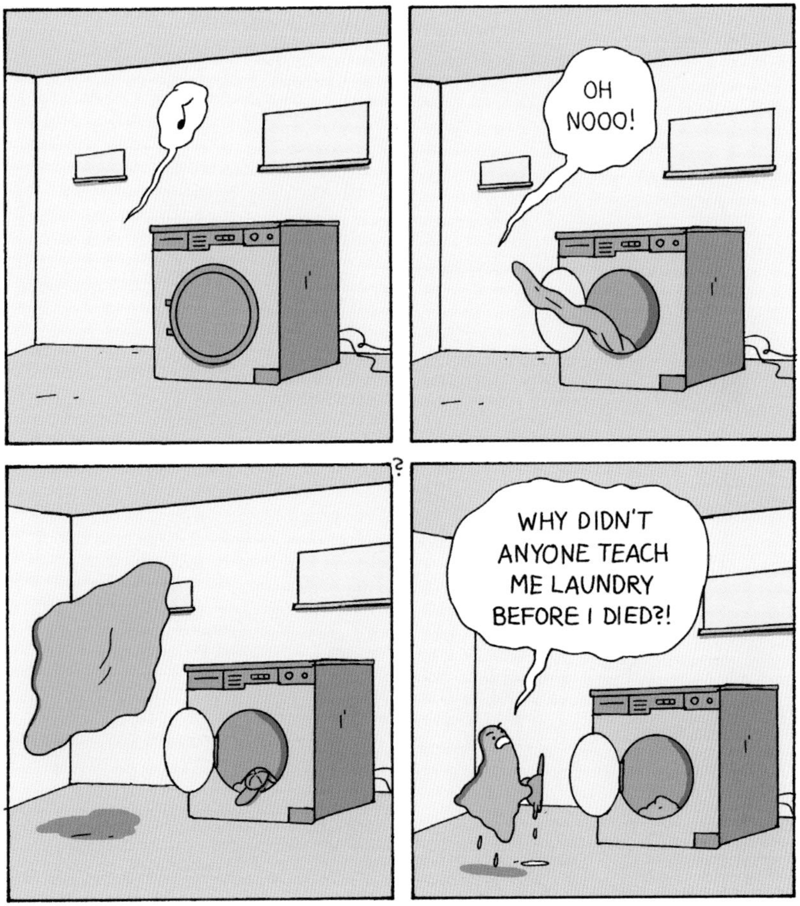

♪
OH NOOO!
?
WHY DIDN'T ANYONE TEACH ME LAUNDRY BEFORE I DIED?!

PERFECT MODEL

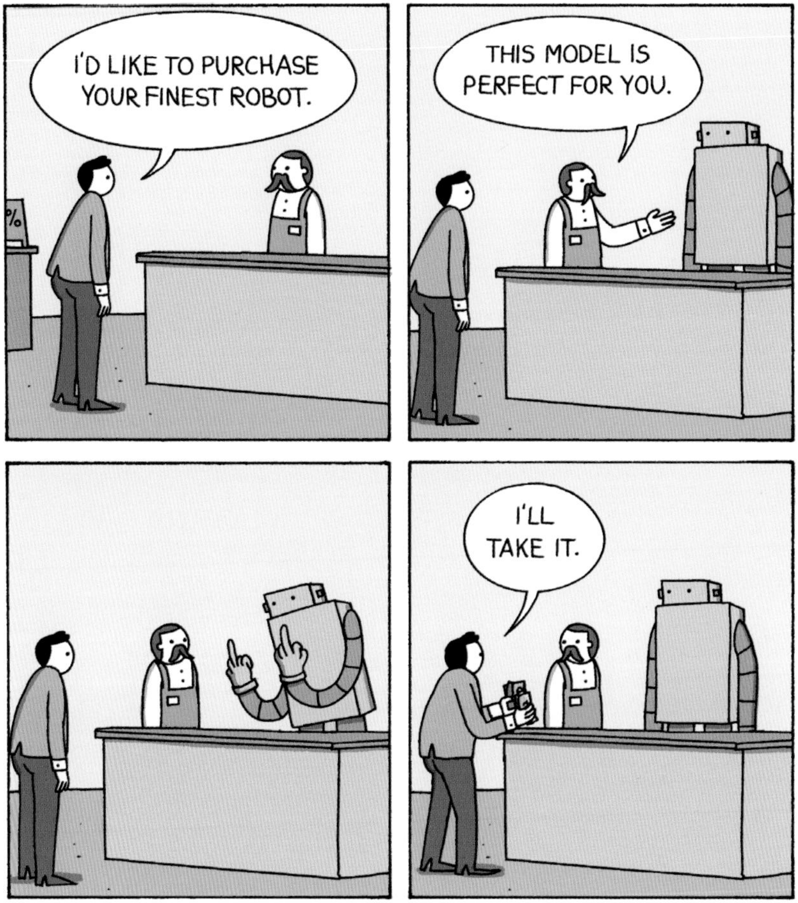
I'D LIKE TO PURCHASE YOUR FINEST ROBOT.
THIS MODEL IS PERFECT FOR YOU.
I'LL TAKE IT.

TIRED OF BEING A GOOD BOY

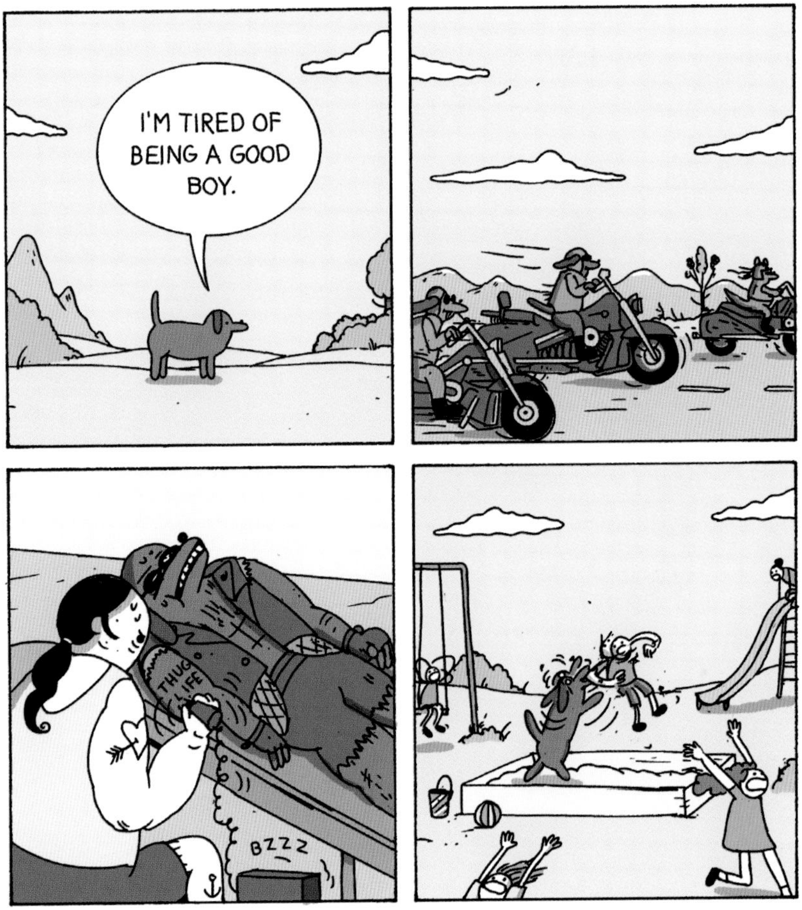
I'M TIRED OF BEING A GOOD BOY.
THUG LIFE
BZZZ

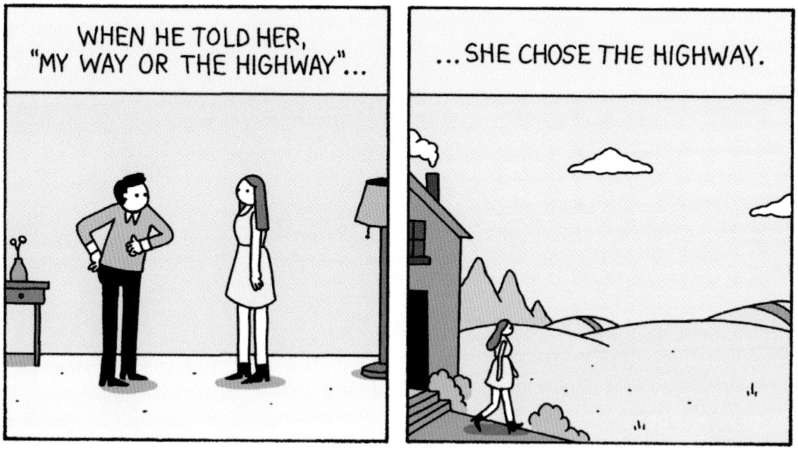
WHEN HE TOLD HER,
"MY WAY OR THE HIGHWAY"...
...SHE CHOSE THE HIGHWAY.

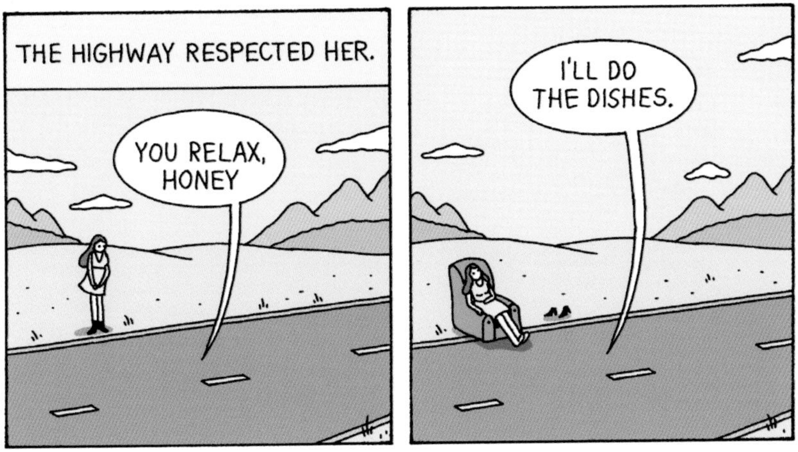
THE HIGHWAY RESPECTED HER.
YOU RELAX, HONEY
I'LL DO THE DISHES.

BATCAVE

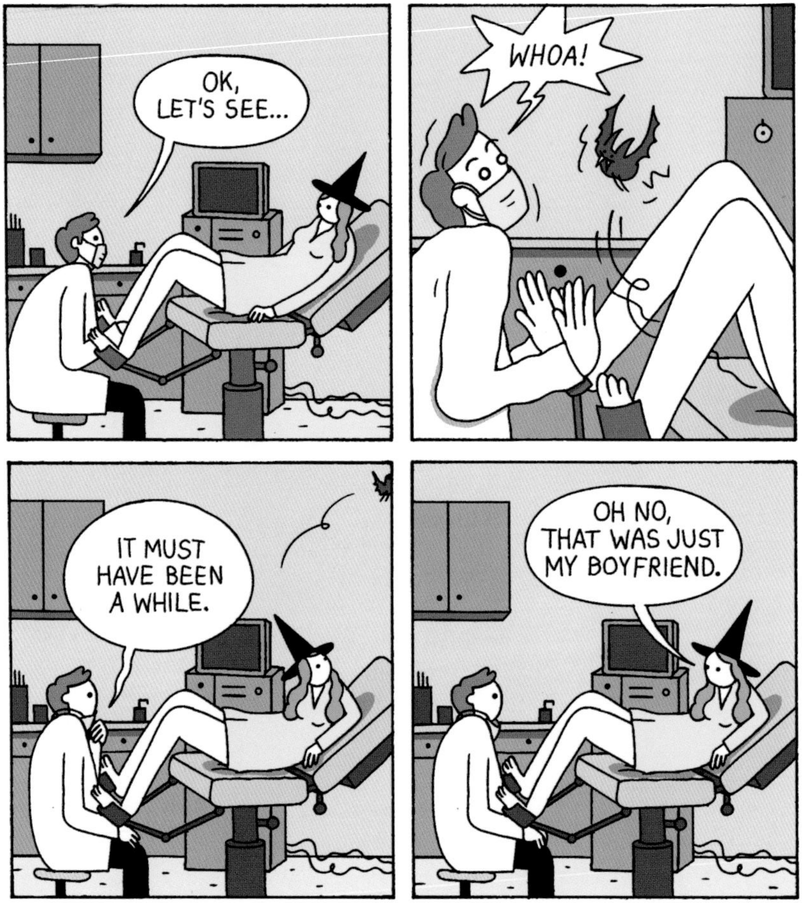
OK, LET'S SEE...
WHOA!
IT MUST HAVE BEEN A WHILE.
OH NO, THAT WAS JUST MY BOYFRIEND.

FATHER'S SHIRT

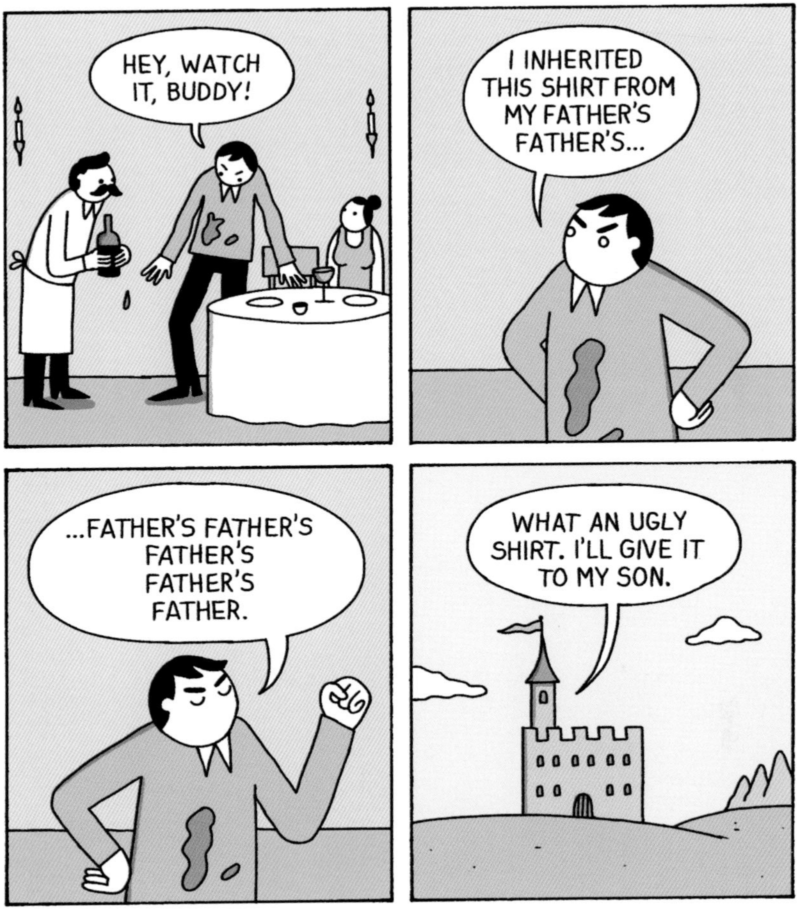
HEY, WATCH IT, BUDDY!
I INHERITED THIS SHIRT FROM MY FATHER'S FATHER'S...
...FATHER'S FATHER'S FATHER'S FATHER'S FATHER.
WHAT AN UGLY SHIRT. I'LL GIVE IT TO MY SON.

ON VACATION

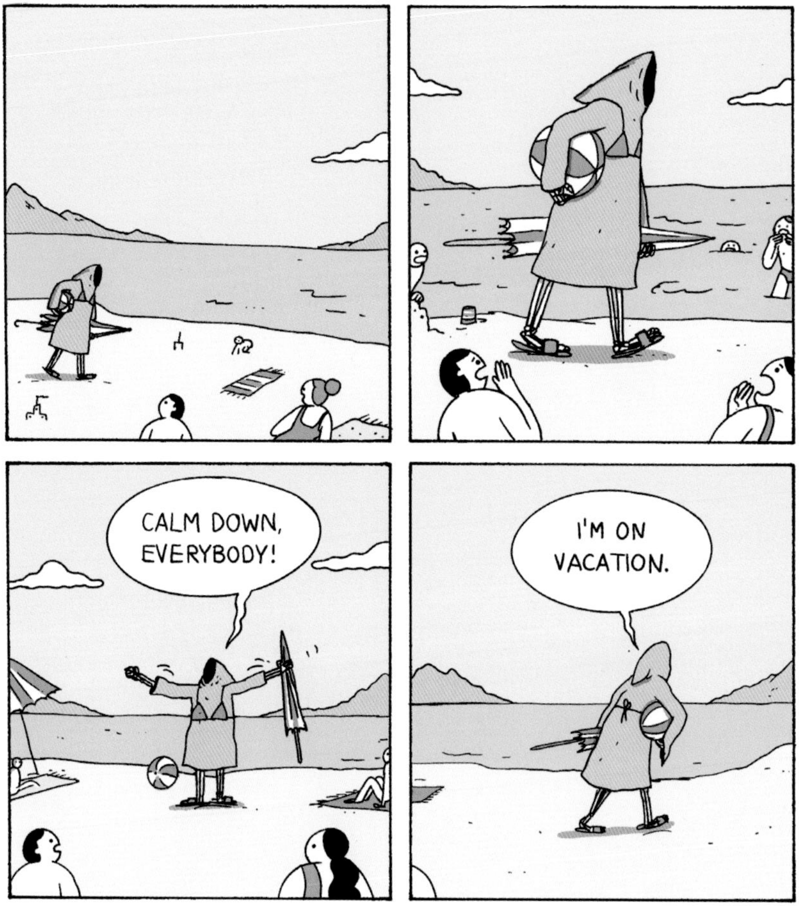
CALM DOWN, EVERYBODY!
I'M ON VACATION.

DOG TRANSLATOR

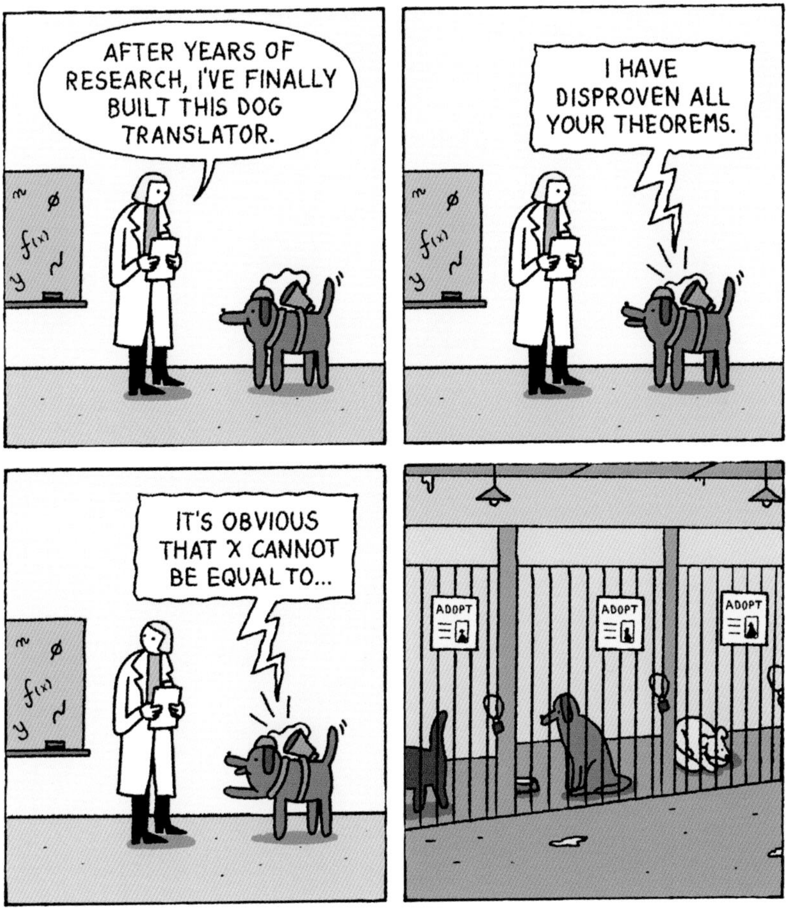
AFTER YEARS OF RESEARCH, I'VE FINALLY BUILT THIS DOG TRANSLATOR.
I HAVE DISPROVEN ALL YOUR THEOREMS.
IT'S OBVIOUS THAT X CANNOT BE EQUAL TO...
ADOPT
ADOPT
ADOPT

DO YOU LOVE ME?

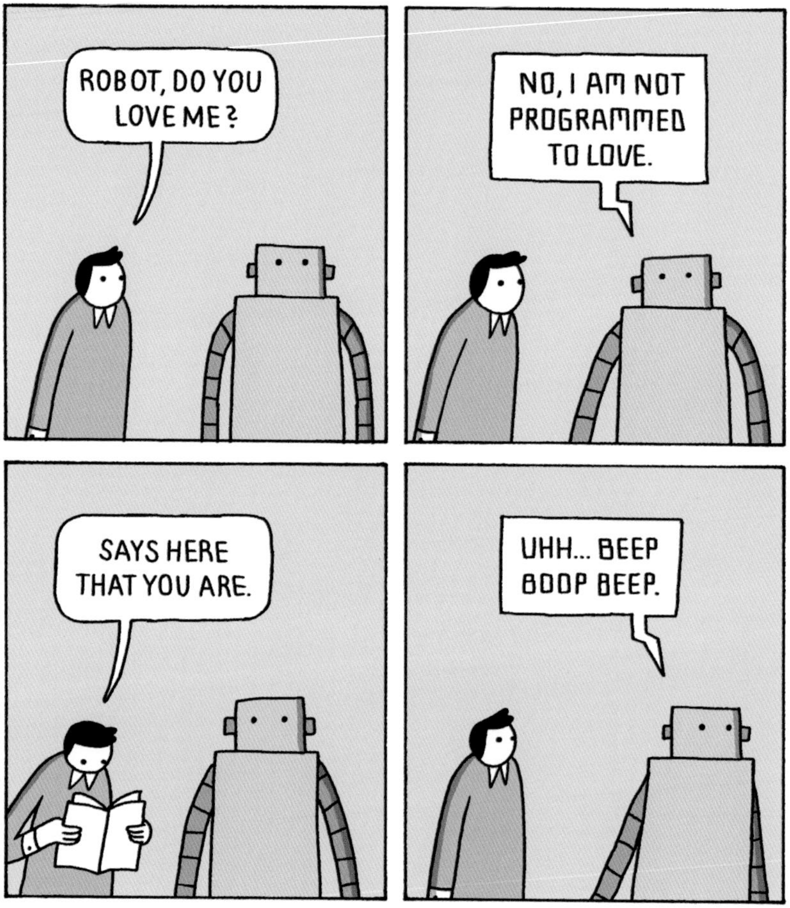
ROBOT, DO YOU LOVE ME?
NO, I AM NOT PROGRAMMED TO LOVE.
SAYS HERE THAT YOU ARE.
UHH... BEEP BOOP BEEP.

REINCARNATION

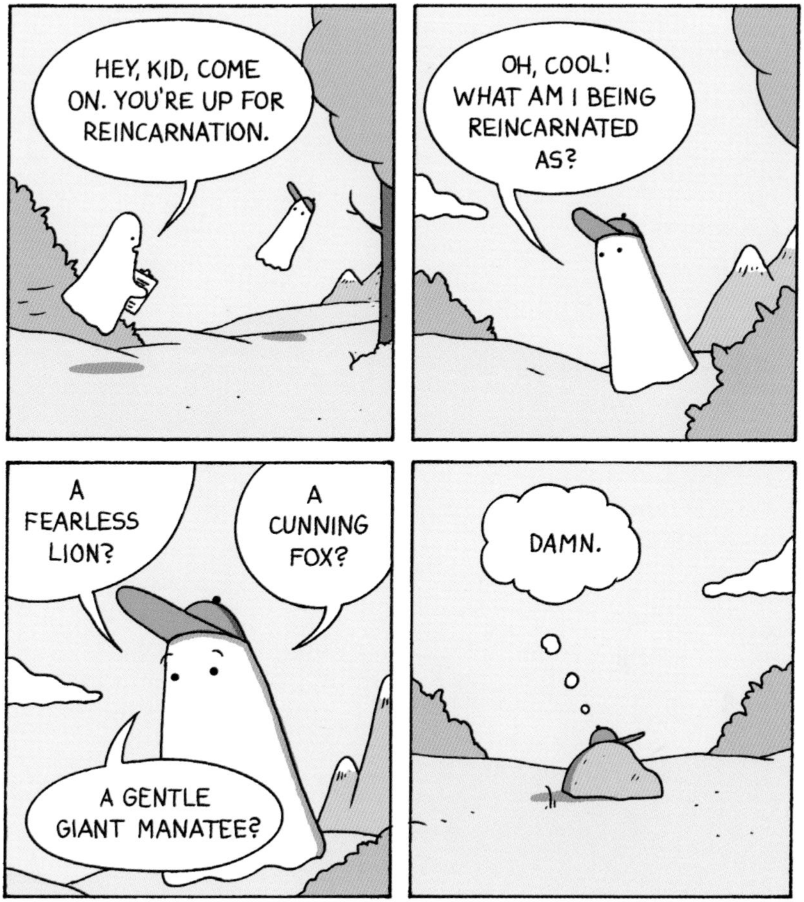
HEY, KID, COME ON. YOU'RE UP FOR REINCARNATION.
OH, COOL! WHAT AM I BEING REINCARNATED AS?
A FEARLESS LION?
A CUNNING FOX?
A GENTLE GIANT MANATEE?
DAMN.

GOOD GIRL

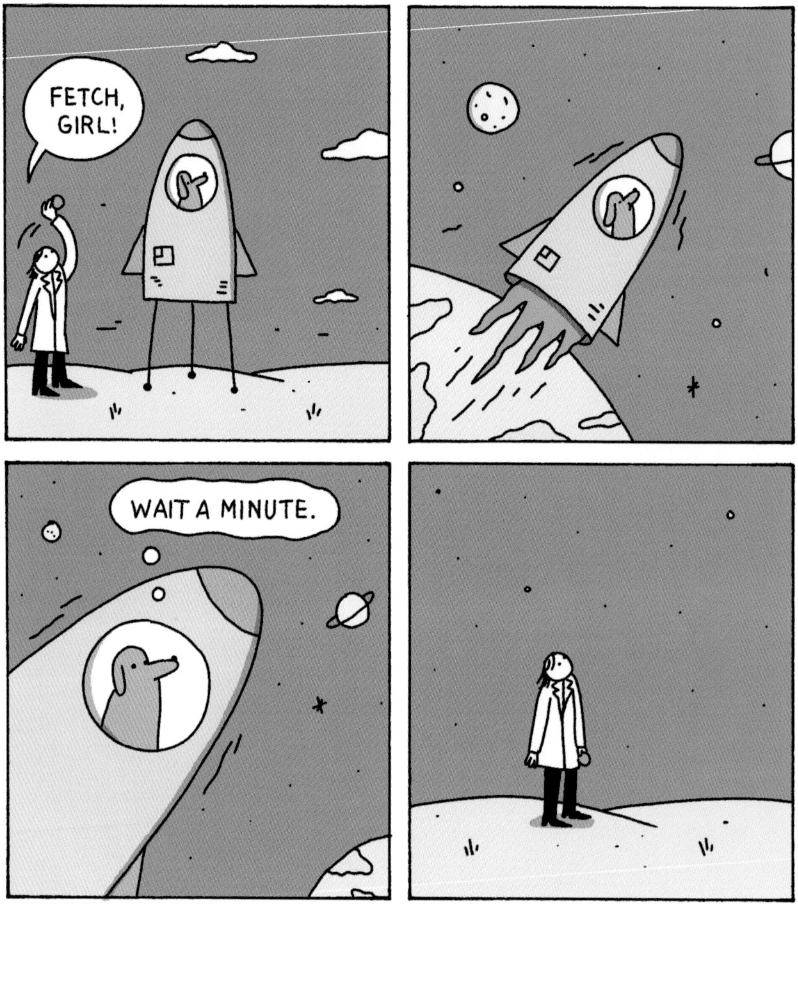
FETCH, GIRL!
WAIT A MINUTE.

On November 3, 1957, a brave astronaut died. Her name was Laika, and she was the first earthly being to orbit our planet.

Rest in peace, you good girl. We'll never forget.

A FEW DRINKS

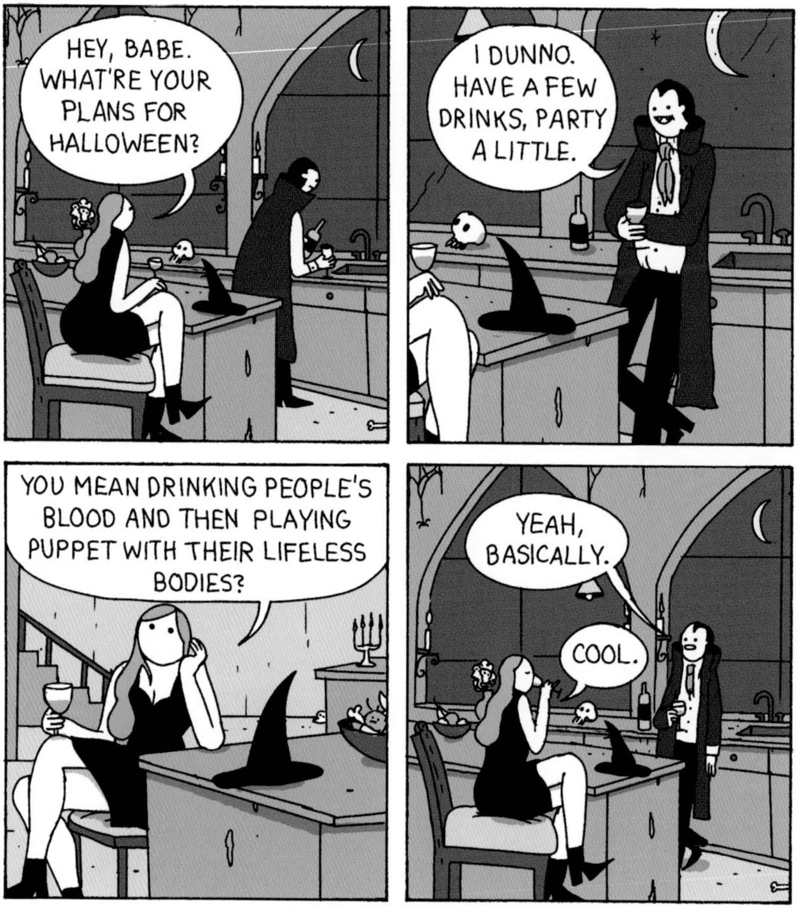
HEY, BABE. WHAT'RE YOUR PLANS FOR HALLOWEEN?
I DUNNO. HAVE A FEW DRINKS, PARTY A LITTLE.
YOU MEAN DRINKING PEOPLE'S BLOOD AND THEN PLAYING PUPPET WITH THEIR LIFELESS BODIES?
YEAH, BASICALLY.
COOL.

YOU LOOK DIFFERENT

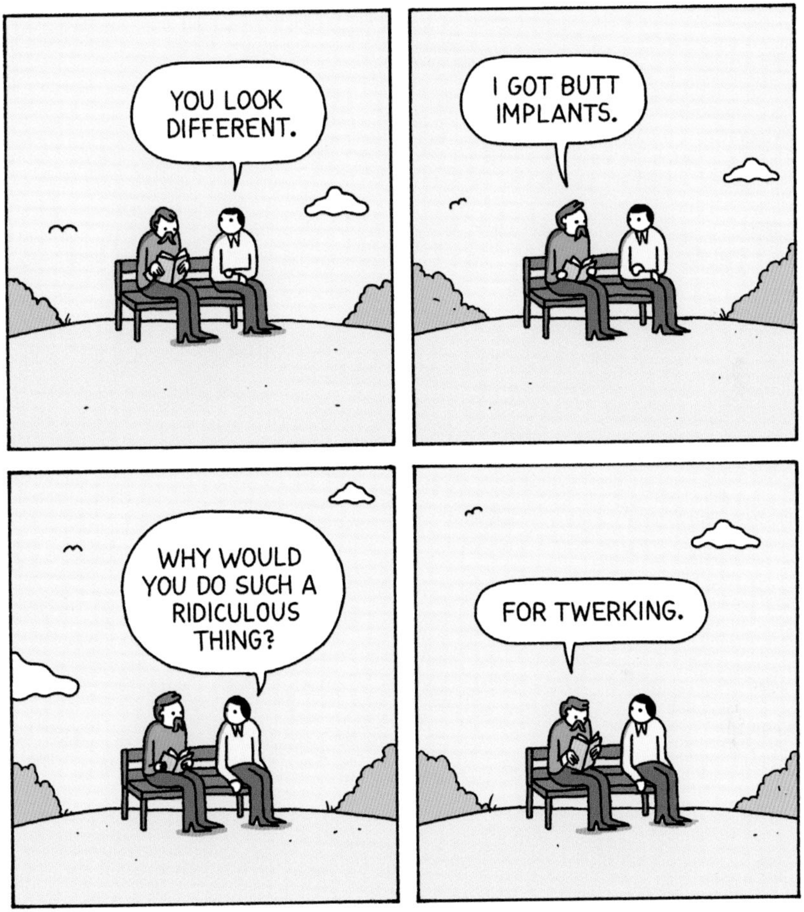

YOU LOOK DIFFERENT.
I GOT BUTT IMPLANTS.
WHY WOULD YOU DO SUCH A RIDICULOUS THING?
FOR TWERKING.

IMMORTALITY

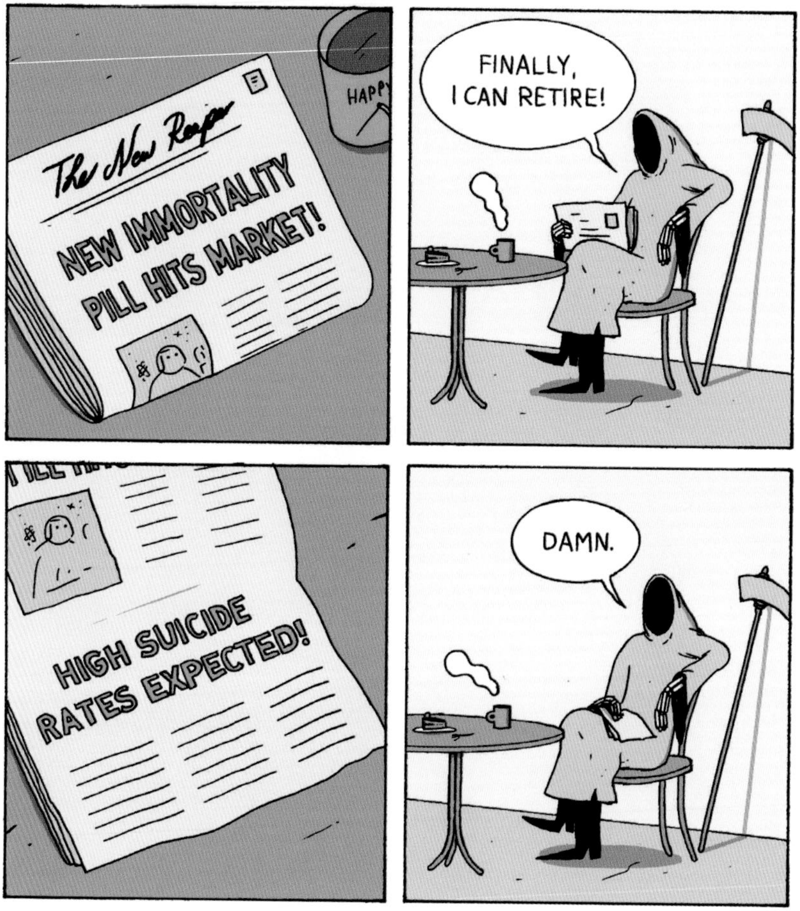
The New Reaper
NEW IMMORTALITY PILL HITS MARKET!
HAPPY
FINALLY, I CAN RETIRE!
HIGH SUICIDE RATES EXPECTED!
DAMN.

CHECK, PLEASE!

I'LL ADMIT, WHEN I AGREED TO THIS DATE, I THOUGHT YOU WERE A HUMAN.
WELL, I'M A VERY GOOD LISTENER...
...AND I HAVE MULTIPLE BODY PARTS THAT CAN VIBRATE.
COULD WE GET THE CHECK, PLEASE?

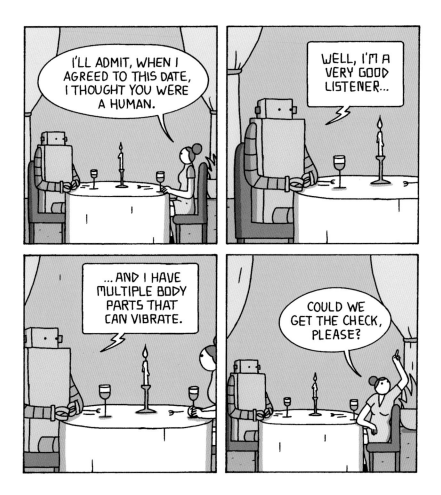

PERSPECTIVE

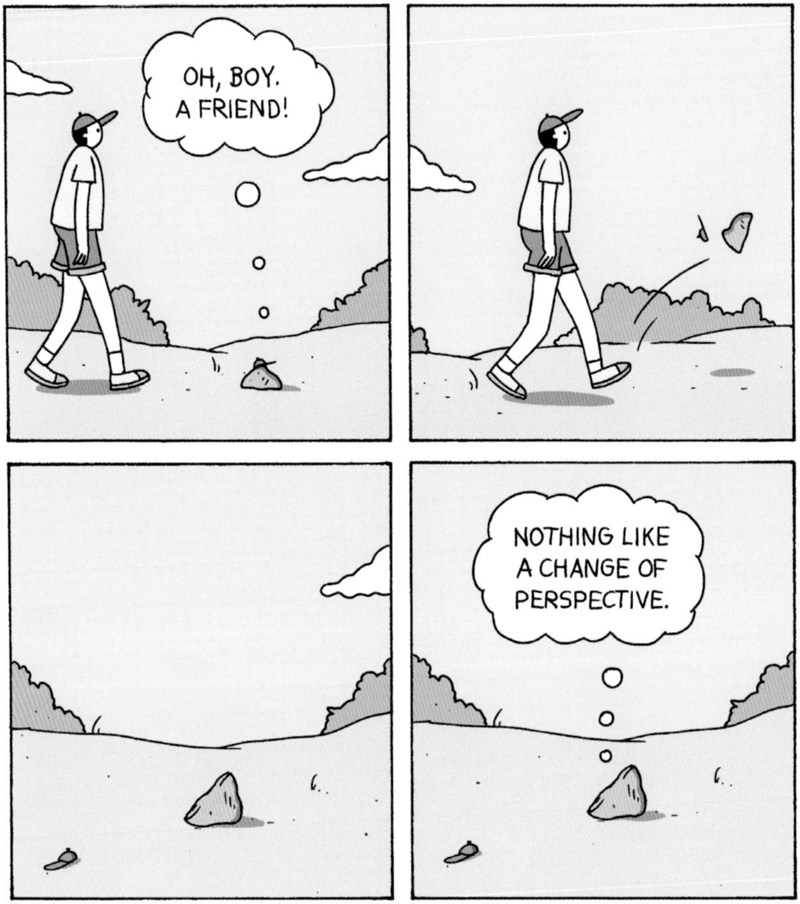
OH, BOY. A FRIEND!
NOTHING LIKE A CHANGE OF PERSPECTIVE.

SWEET BABY

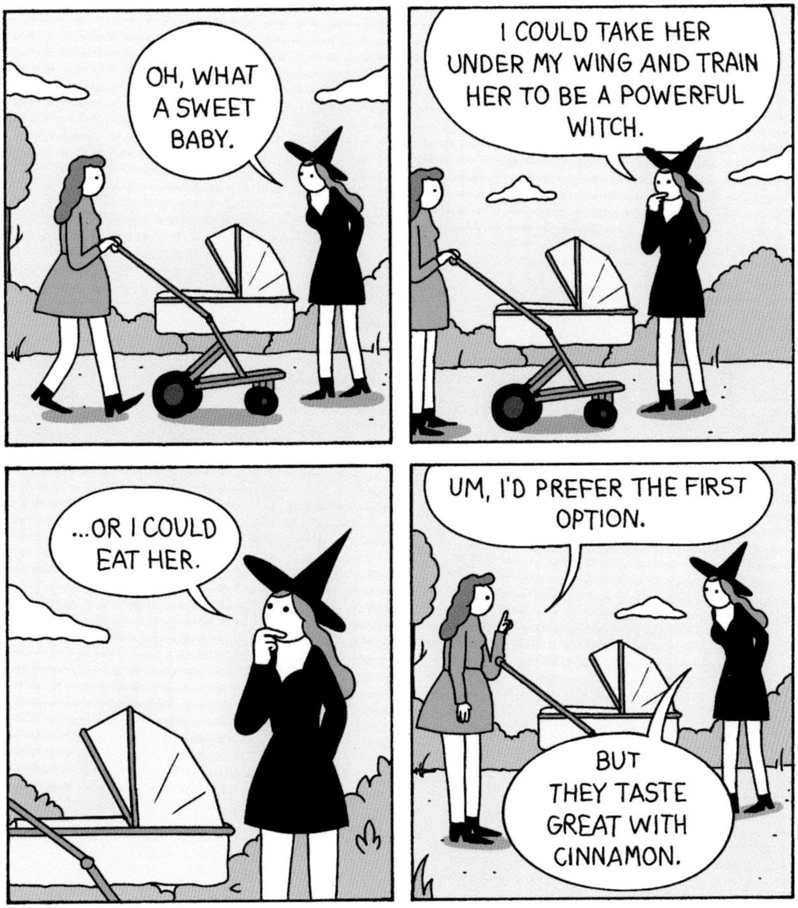

OH, WHAT A SWEET BABY.
I COULD TAKE HER UNDER MY WING AND TRAIN HER TO BE A POWERFUL WITCH.
...OR I COULD EAT HER.
UM, I'D PREFER THE FIRST OPTION.
BUT THEY TASTE GREAT WITH CINNAMON.

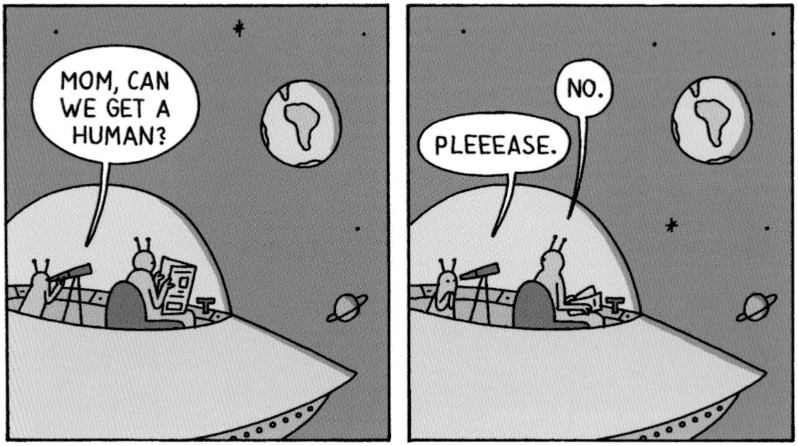
MOM, CAN WE GET A HUMAN?
PLEEEASE.
NO.

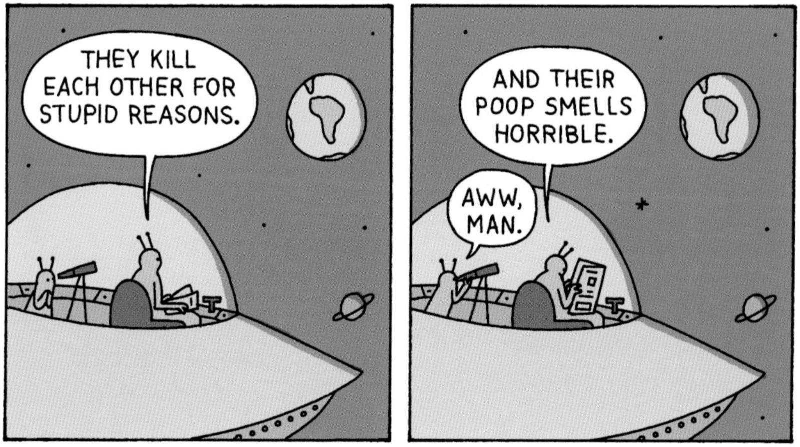
THEY KILL EACH OTHER FOR STUPID REASONS.
AND THEIR POOP SMELLS HORRIBLE.
AWW, MAN.

LASERS

AHAHAH
NIBBLES, BE HONEST... WHY DO YOU REALLY HANG OUT WITH ME?
WHAT DO YOU MEAN? YOU'RE MY FRIEND AND I LOVE YOU VERY MUCH.
BUT LET'S KEEP THOSE LASERS COMING.

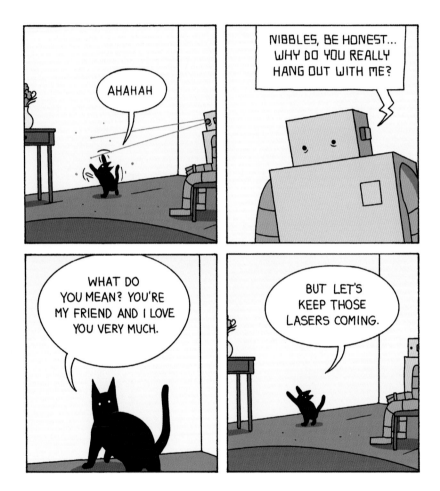

OBVIOUSLY

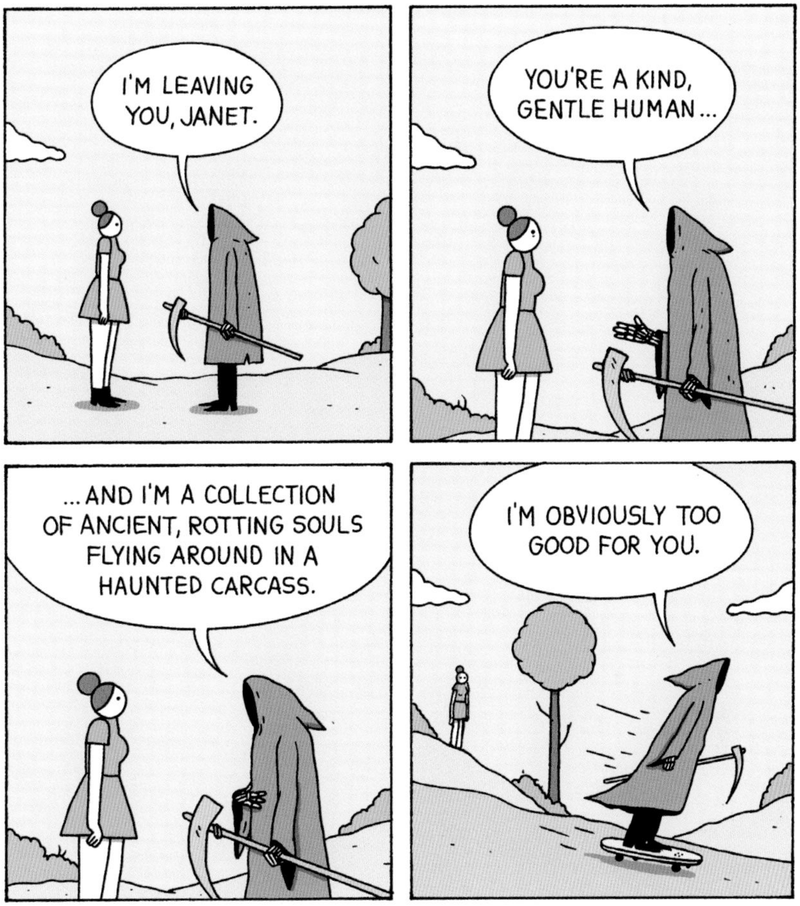
I'M LEAVING YOU, JANET.
YOU'RE A KIND, GENTLE HUMAN...
...AND I'M A COLLECTION OF ANCIENT, ROTTING SOULS FLYING AROUND IN A HAUNTED CARCASS.
I'M OBVIOUSLY TOO GOOD FOR YOU.

SICK BURN

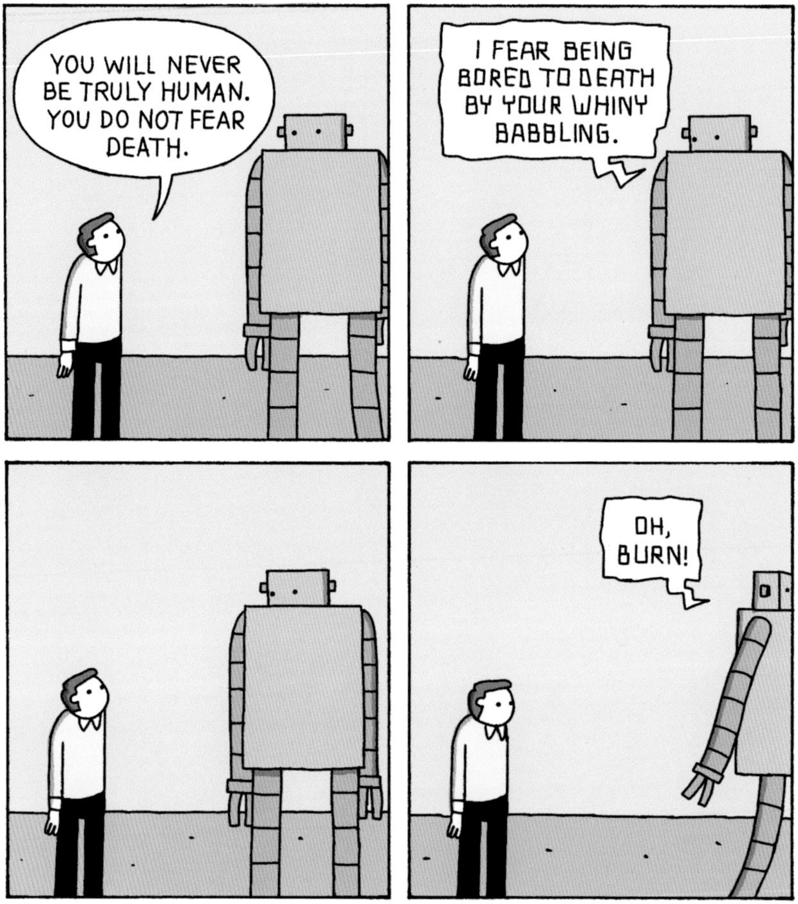
YOU WILL NEVER BE TRULY HUMAN. YOU DO NOT FEAR DEATH.
I FEAR BEING BORED TO DEATH BY YOUR WHINY BABBLING.
OH, BURN!

COVEN GOALS

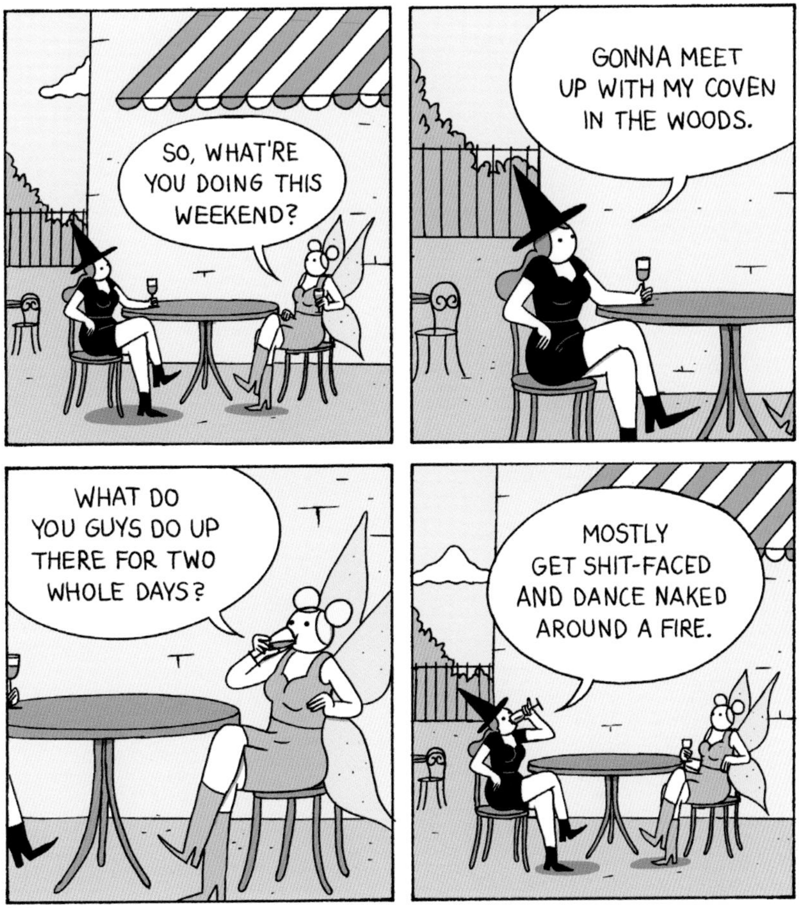
SO, WHAT'RE YOU DOING THIS WEEKEND?
GONNA MEET UP WITH MY COVEN IN THE WOODS.
WHAT DO YOU GUYS DO UP THERE FOR TWO WHOLE DAYS?
MOSTLY GET SHIT-FACED AND DANCE NAKED AROUND A FIRE.

TO MAXIMIZE CUTENESS, WE ROLL ON OUR BACK AND PRESENT THE FLUFFY BELLY.
HUMA
101
YES, TODD?
WHEN THEY PET US, WHAT DO WE DO?

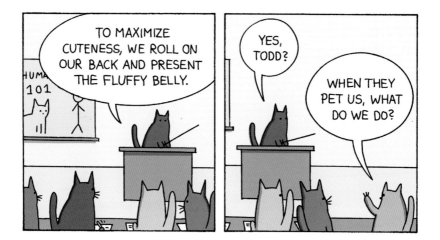

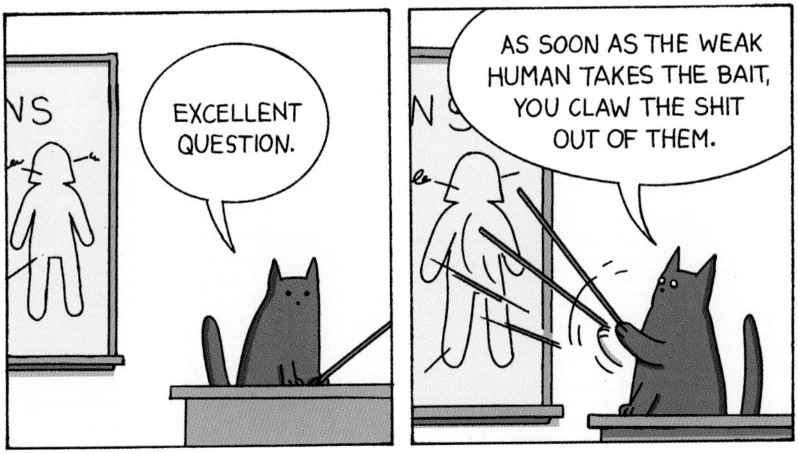

NS
EXCELLENT QUESTION.
NS
AS SOON AS THE WEAK HUMAN TAKES THE BAIT, YOU CLAW THE SHIT OUT OF THEM.

VIRTUAL REALITY

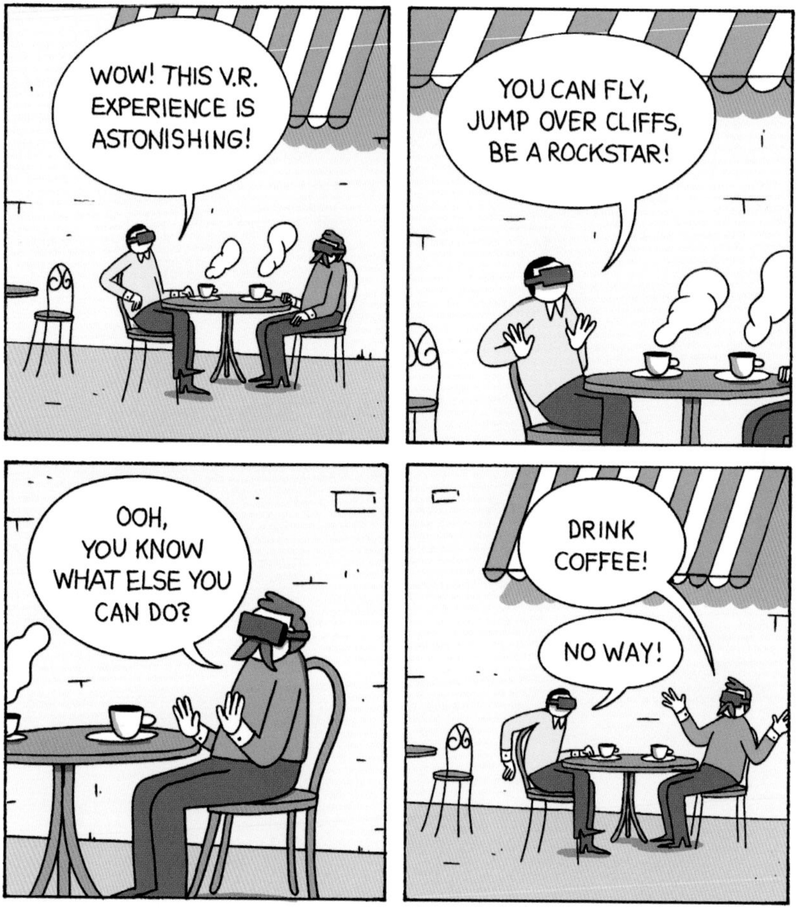
WOW! THIS V.R. EXPERIENCE IS ASTONISHING!
YOU CAN FLY, JUMP OVER CLIFFS, BE A ROCKSTAR!
OOH, YOU KNOW WHAT ELSE YOU CAN DO?
DRINK COFFEE!
NO WAY!

NOT SO GRIM

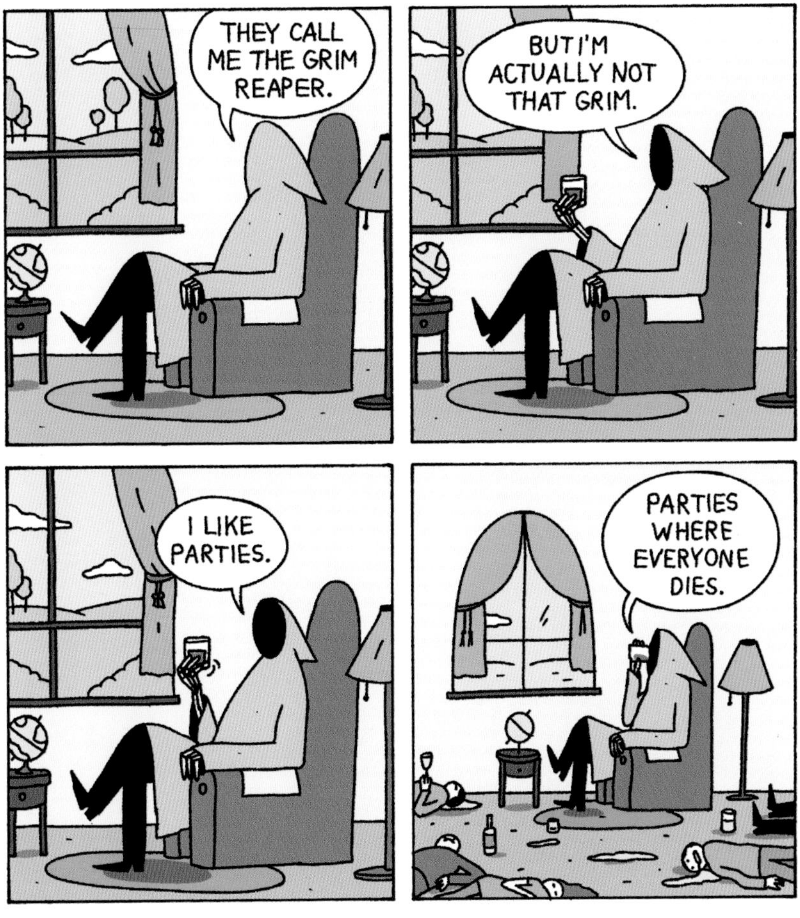
THEY CALL ME THE GRIM REAPER.
BUT I'M ACTUALLY NOT THAT GRIM.
I LIKE PARTIES.
PARTIES WHERE EVERYONE DIES.

FAT32

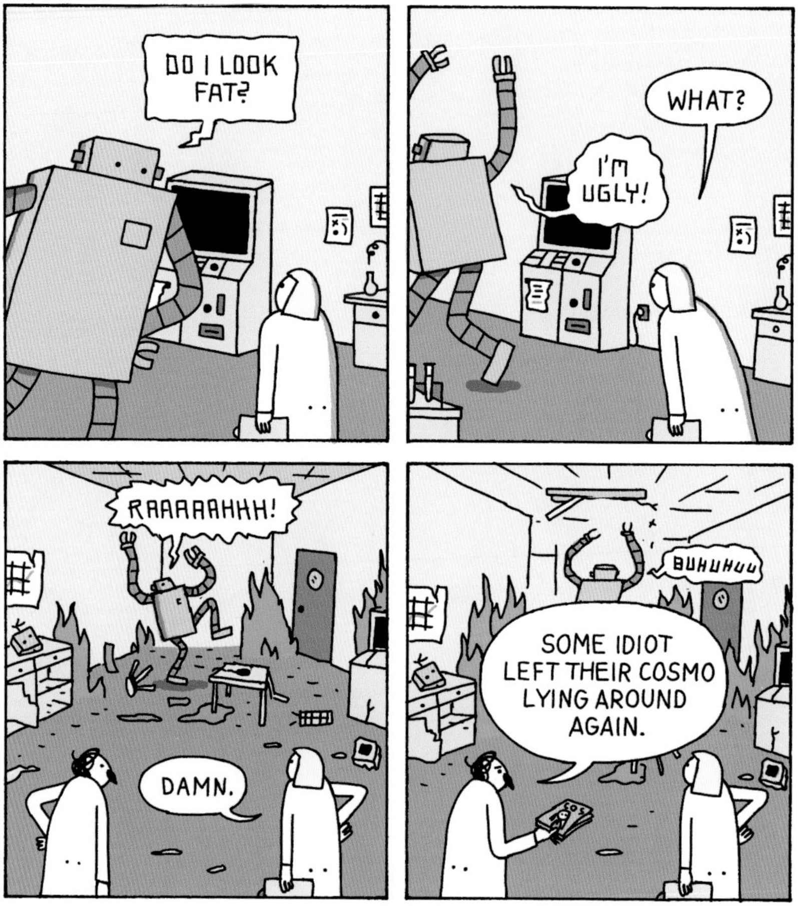
DO I LOOK FAT?
WHAT?
I'M UGLY!
RAAAAAHHH!
DAMN.
BUHUHUU
SOME IDIOT LEFT THEIR COSMO LYING AROUND AGAIN.

ANYTHING

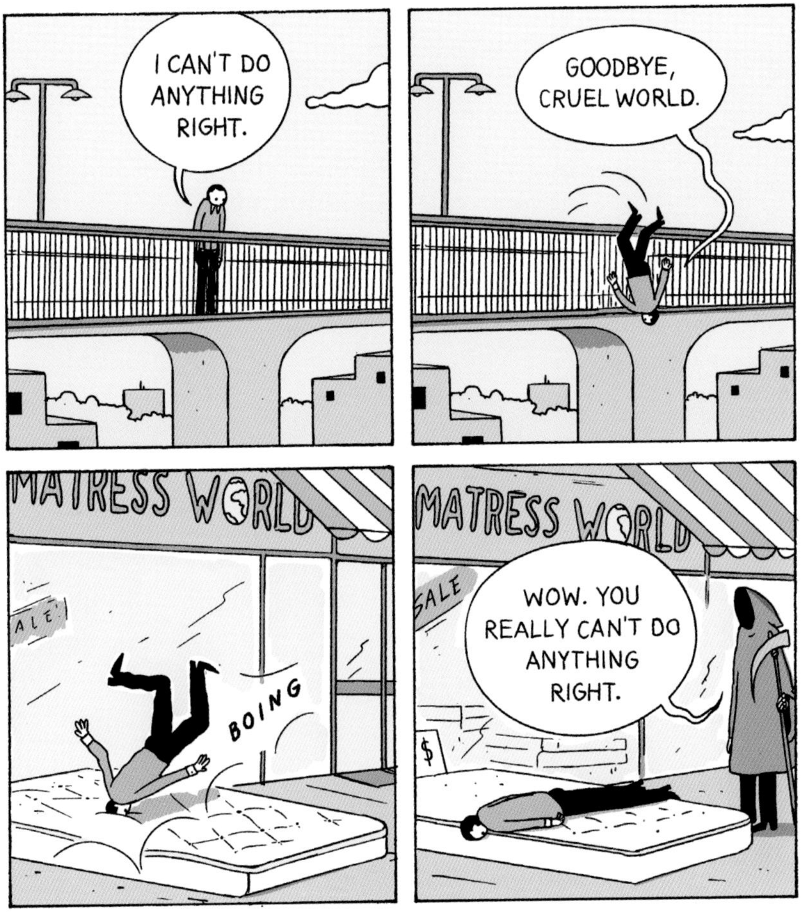
I CAN'T DO ANYTHING RIGHT.
GOODBYE, CRUEL WORLD.
MATRESS WORLD
BOING
MATRESS WORLD
SALE
WOW. YOU REALLY CAN'T DO ANYTHING RIGHT.

SIGH

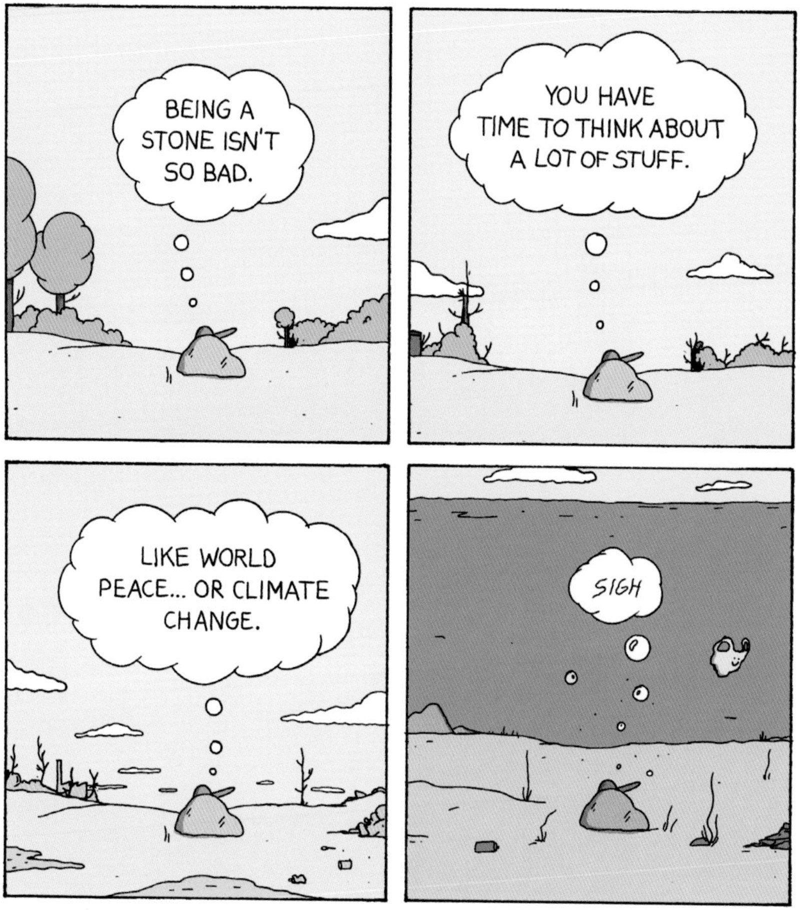
BEING A STONE ISN'T SO BAD.
YOU HAVE TIME TO THINK ABOUT A LOT OF STUFF.
LIKE WORLD PEACE... OR CLIMATE CHANGE.
SIGH

VIBRATION MODE

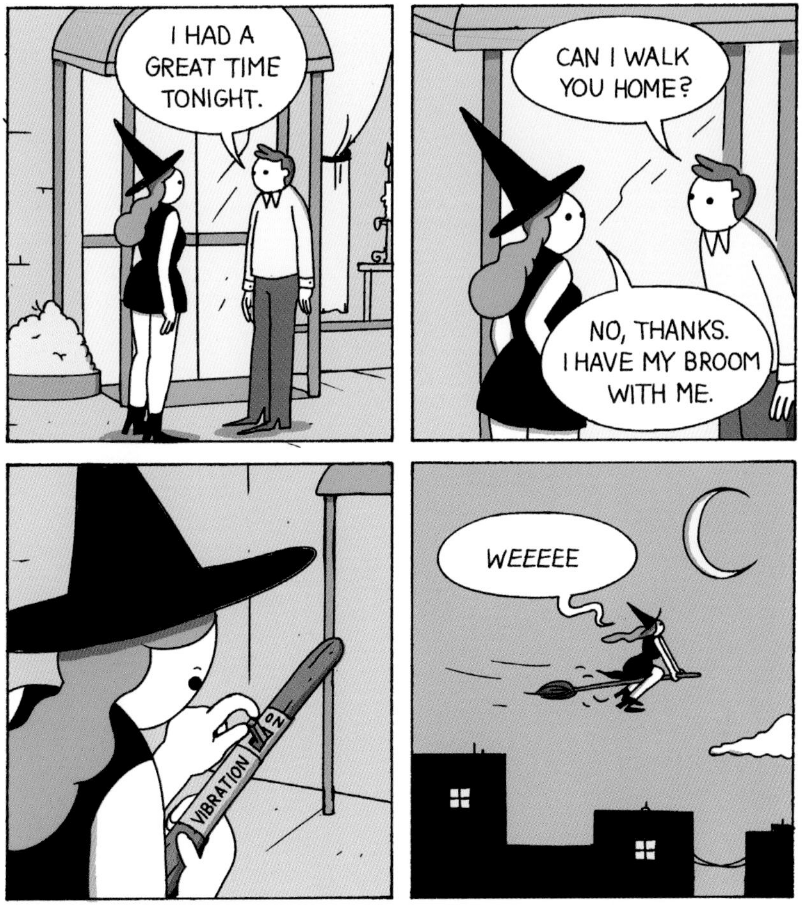
I HAD A GREAT TIME TONIGHT.
CAN I WALK YOU HOME?
NO, THANKS. I HAVE MY BROOM WITH ME.
VIBRATION
ON
WEEEEE

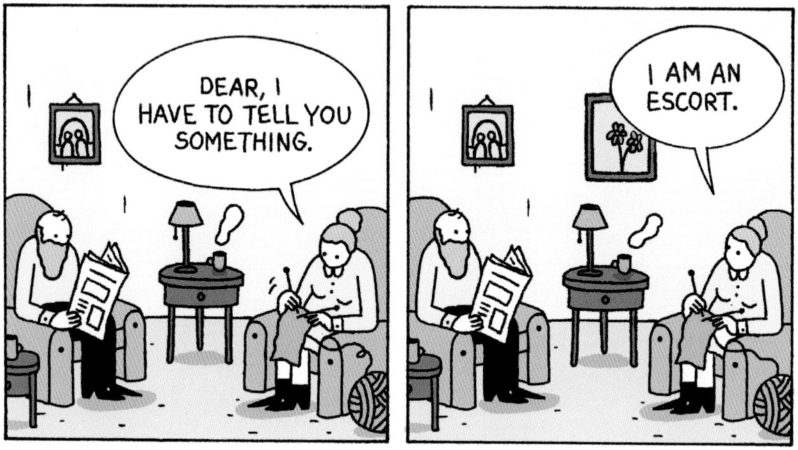
DEAR, I HAVE TO TELL YOU SOMETHING.
I AM AN ESCORT.

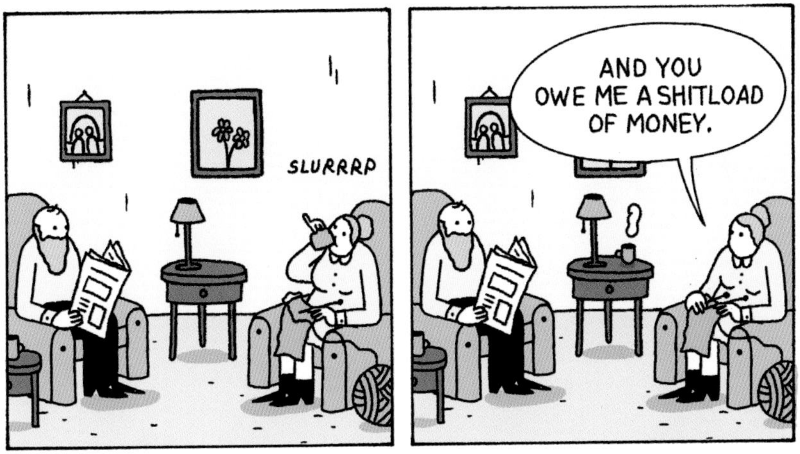
SLURRRP
AND YOU OWE ME A SHITLOAD OF MONEY.

REAPER'S DELIGHT

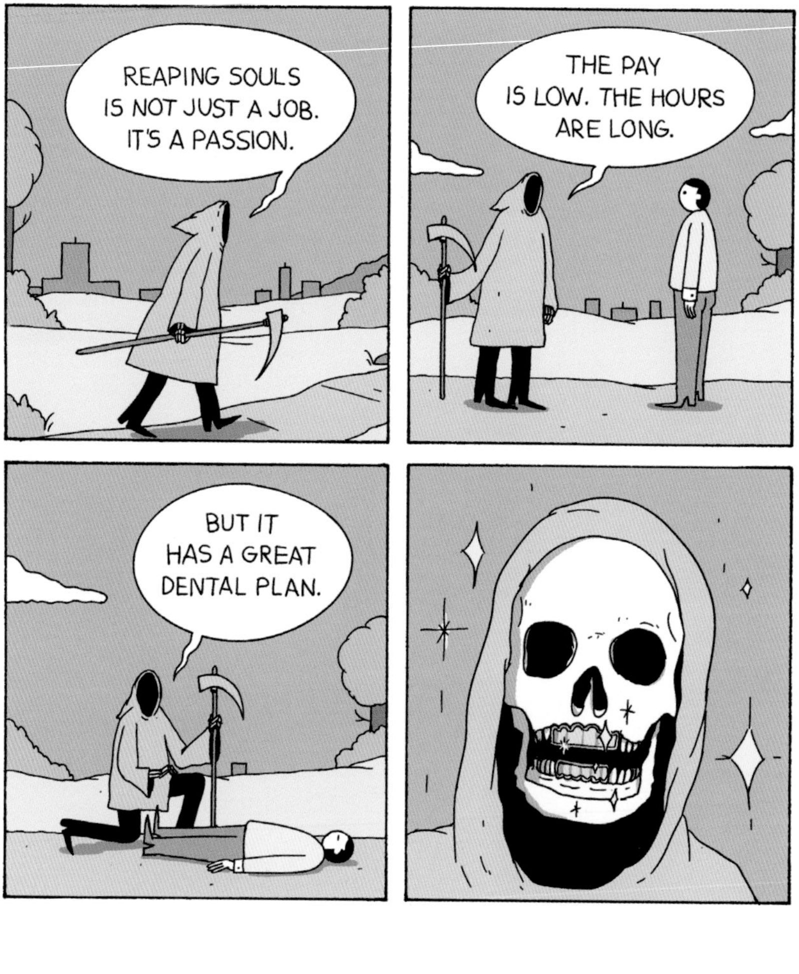
REAPING SOULS IS NOT JUST A JOB. IT'S A PASSION.
THE PAY IS LOW. THE HOURS ARE LONG.
BUT IT HAS A GREAT DENTAL PLAN.

GIRLS' NIGHT

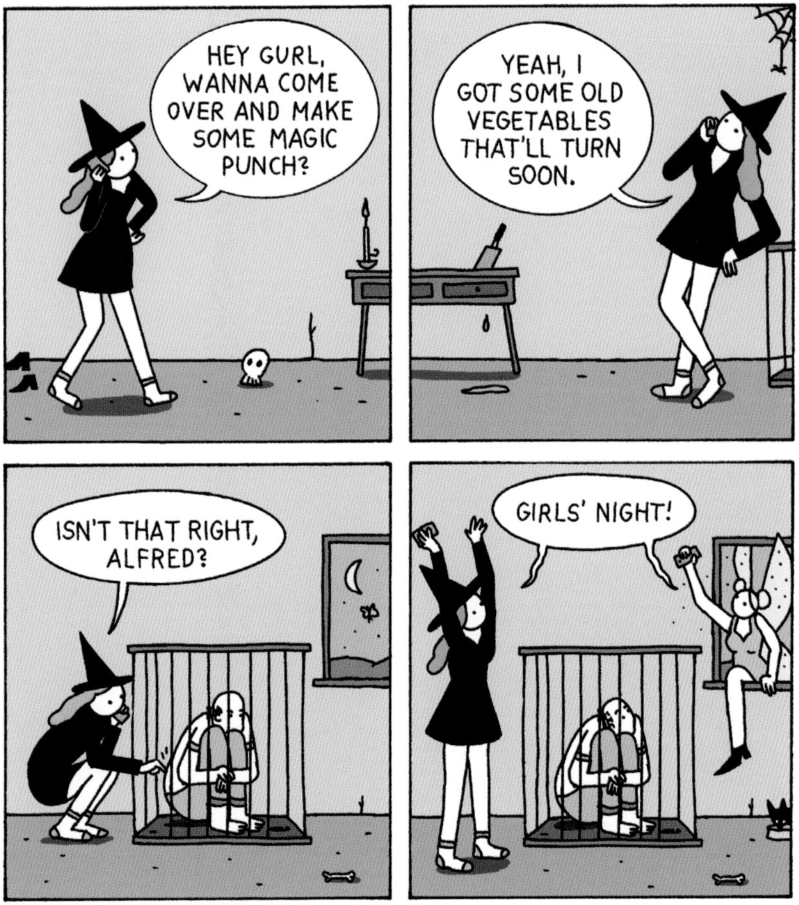
HEY GURL, WANNA COME OVER AND MAKE SOME MAGIC PUNCH?
YEAH, I GOT SOME OLD VEGETABLES THAT'LL TURN SOON.
ISN'T THAT RIGHT, ALFRED?
GIRLS' NIGHT!

PRINTERS

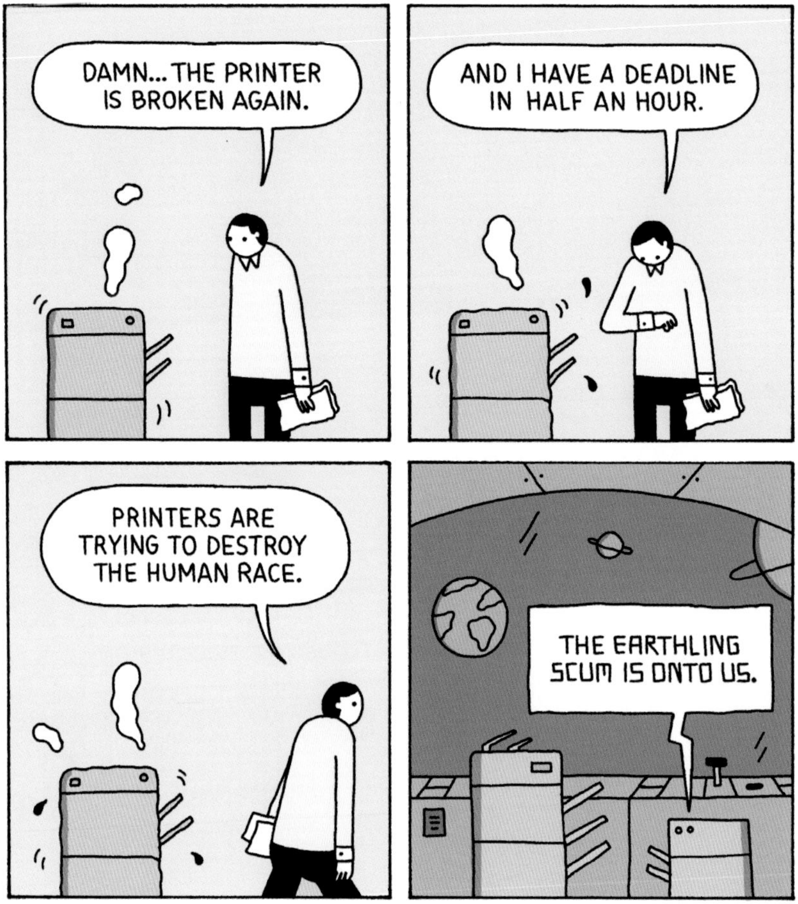
DAMN... THE PRINTER IS BROKEN AGAIN.
AND I HAVE A DEADLINE IN HALF AN HOUR.
PRINTERS ARE TRYING TO DESTROY THE HUMAN RACE.
THE EARTHLING SCUM IS ONTO US.

BEAUTIFUL DREAM

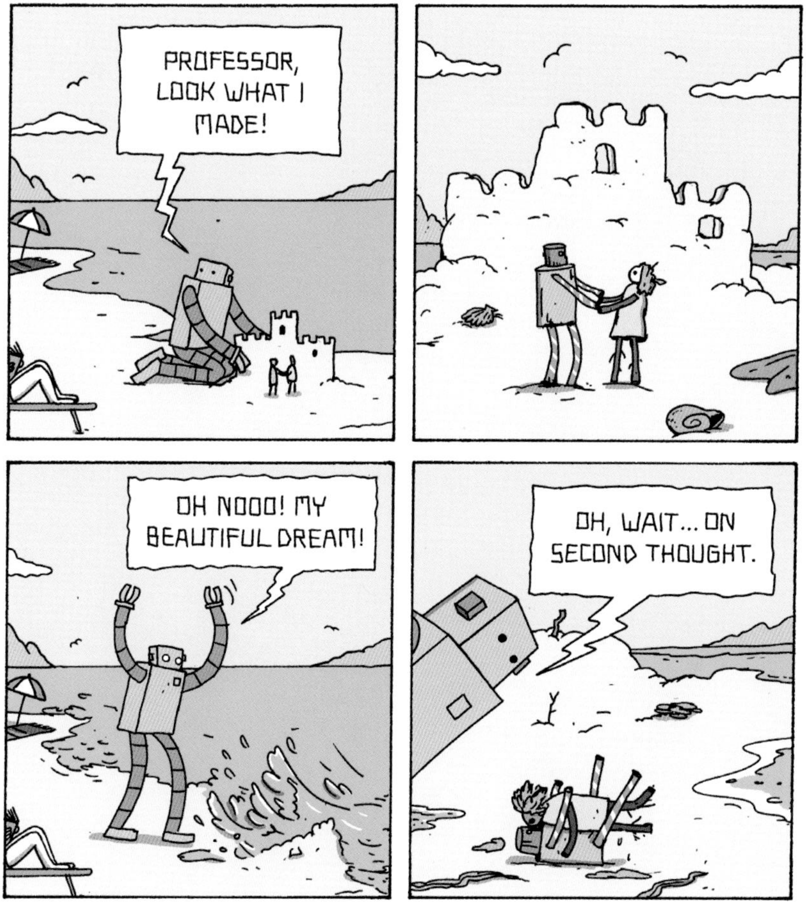
PROFESSOR, LOOK WHAT I MADE!
OH NOOO! MY BEAUTIFUL DREAM!
OH, WAIT... ON SECOND THOUGHT.

NOBODY

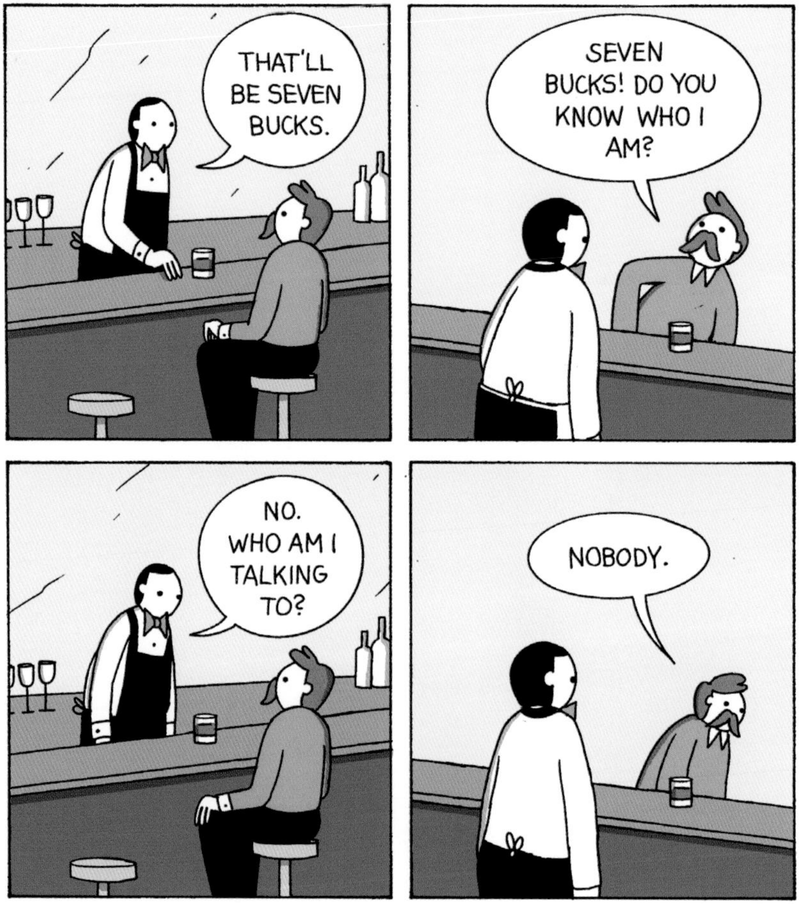

THAT'LL BE SEVEN BUCKS.
SEVEN BUCKS! DO YOU KNOW WHO I AM?
NO. WHO AM I TALKING TO?
NOBODY.

WHOLESOME WITCH

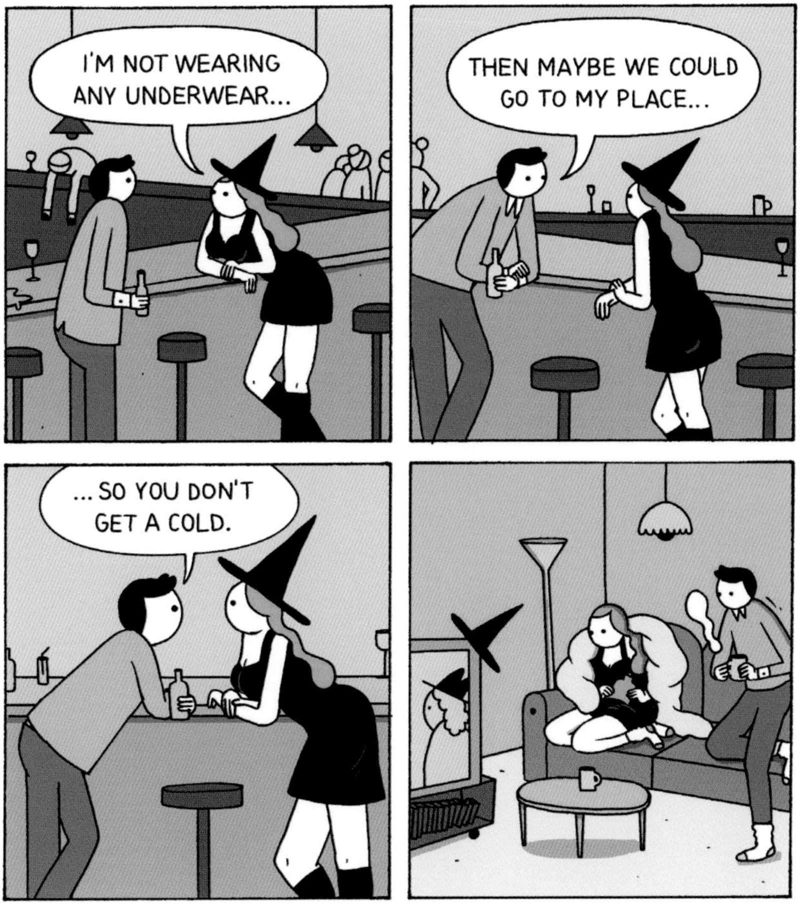
I'M NOT WEARING ANY UNDERWEAR...
THEN MAYBE WE COULD GO TO MY PLACE...
...SO YOU DON'T GET A COLD.

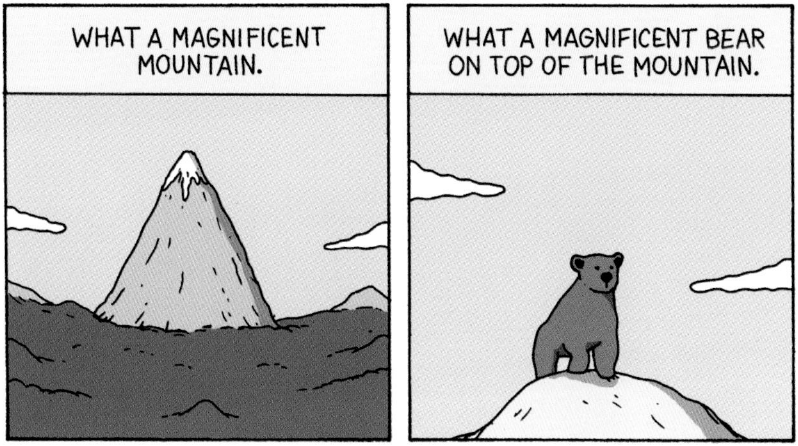
WHAT A MAGNIFICENT MOUNTAIN.
WHAT A MAGNIFICENT BEAR ON TOP OF THE MOUNTAIN.

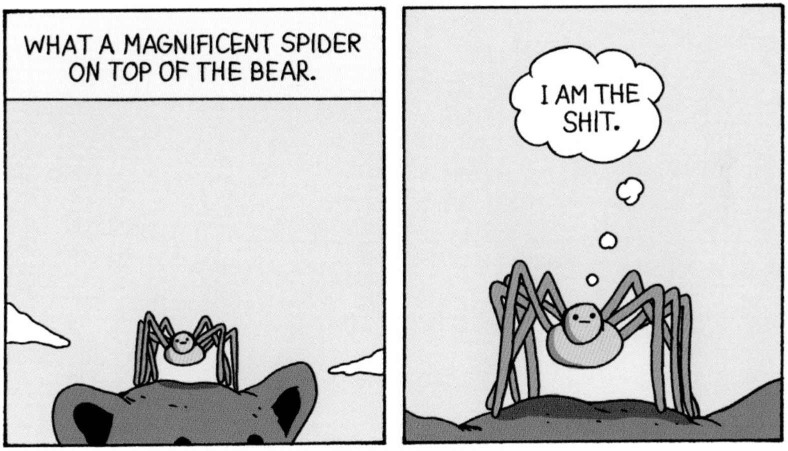
WHAT A MAGNIFICENT SPIDER ON TOP OF THE BEAR.
I AM THE SHIT.

NEXT LEVEL

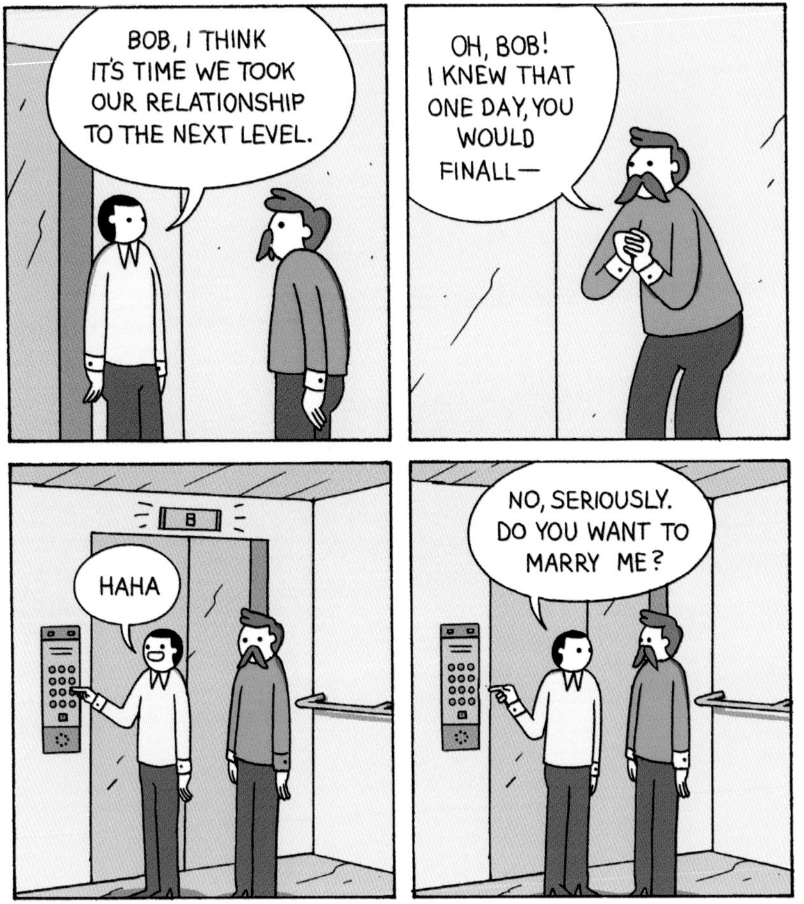
BOB, I THINK IT'S TIME WE TOOK OUR RELATIONSHIP TO THE NEXT LEVEL.
OH, BOB! I KNEW THAT ONE DAY, YOU WOULD FINALL—
HAHA
NO, SERIOUSLY. DO YOU WANT TO MARRY ME?

DEATH-LIFE BALANCE

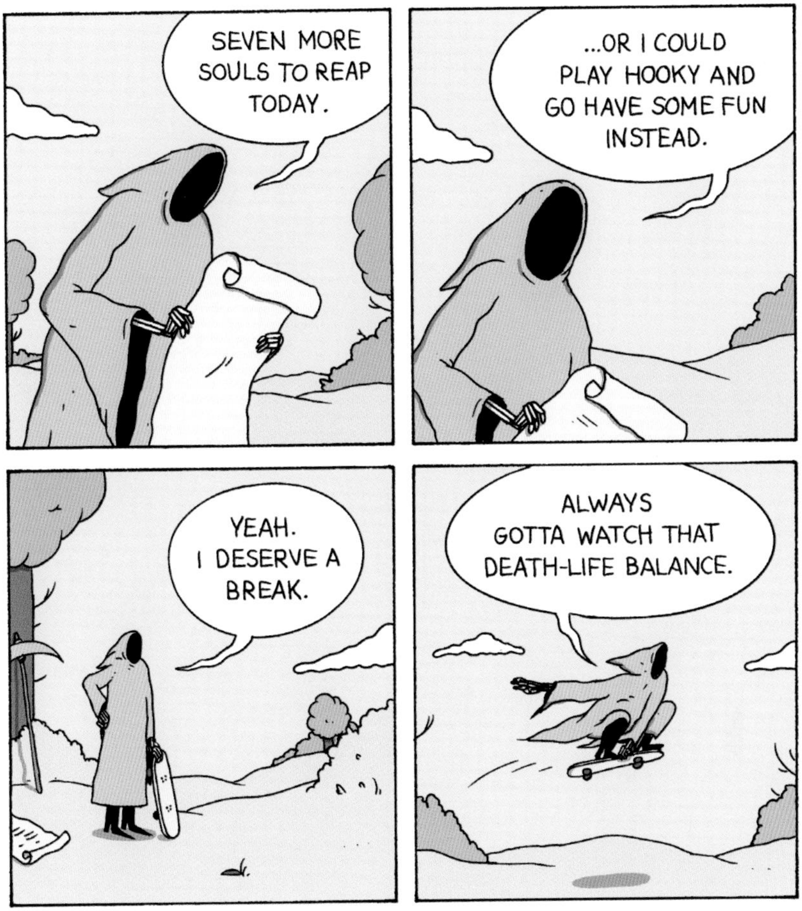

SEVEN MORE SOULS TO REAP TODAY.
...OR I COULD PLAY HOOKY AND GO HAVE SOME FUN INSTEAD.
YEAH. I DESERVE A BREAK.
ALWAYS GOTTA WATCH THAT DEATH-LIFE BALANCE.

LOVE MODULE

PROFESSOR, I'M TIRED OF LOVING YOU AND WAITING FOR YOU TO LOVE ME BACK.
CLICK
WOW, I FEEL NOTHING. THAT WAS EASY.
FOR YOU IT IS.

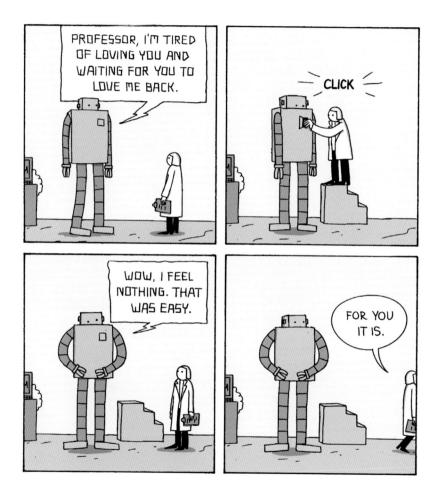

NEW BEGINNING

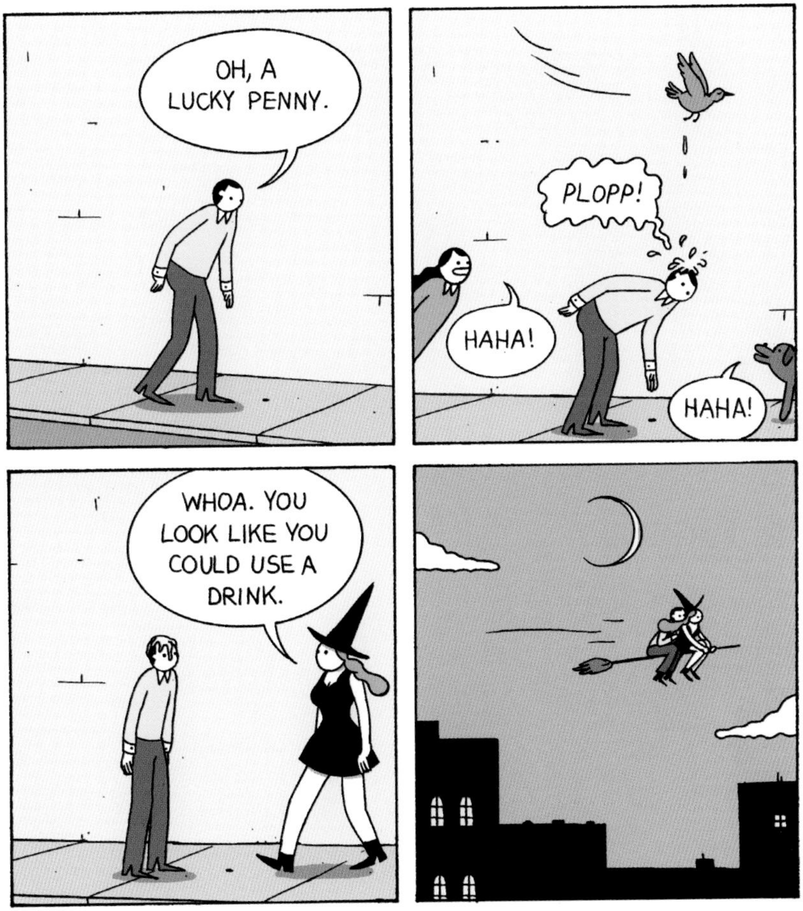
OH, A LUCKY PENNY.
PLOPP!
HAHA!
HAHA!
WHOA. YOU LOOK LIKE YOU COULD USE A DRINK.

ABOUT THE AUTHORS

Jonathan and Elizabeth met in their first year at art school, where they both went to disappoint their parents, who had hoped they would become lawyers or doctors. Instead, they fell madly in love with comics and started making weekly strips on their blog, which would later become the much-loved **War and Peas** (www.warandpeas.com).

With new comics released every week since 2011, *War and Peas* has aquired hundreds of thousands of readers from all over the world. In spite of their success, the two comic artists are hardly recognized in public, allowing them to go on living as they are accustomed: sneaking into art openings and snagging free pastries.

Jonathan and Elizabeth would like to thank:

Barbara Yelin, Anita Ettinger & Thomas Kunz, Eva LeWinter, Nick Seluk, David Daneman, Hartmut Wagner, Ivica Maksimovic, Nicola Barr, Lucas Wetzel, Sarah Andersen, and all their wonderful friends.

They also want to show their appreciation for their patrons, who support them at www.patreon.com/warandpeas:

Csaba Nilgesz, Alex, J' May, Allie Curry, Nils von Carlowitz, Joseph Roberts, Zarko Zobenica, Rebecca Morris, Alice Triolet, Benjamin Garcia, Guiliana Lombardo, and Jessi Burg.

War and Peas copyright © 2020 by Jonathan Kunz and Elizabeth Pich. All rights reserved. Printed in China. No part of this book may be used or reproduced in any manner whatsoever without written permission except in the case of reprints in the context of reviews.

Andrews McMeel Publishing
a division of Andrews McMeel Universal
1130 Walnut Street, Kansas City, Missouri 64106

www.andrewsmcmeel.com

www.warandpeas.com

20 21 22 23 24 SDB 10 9 8 7 6 5 4 3 2 1

ISBN: 978-1-5248-5407-2

Library of Congress Control Number: 2019949900

Editor: Lucas Wetzel
Art Director: Spencer Williams
Production Editor: Jasmine Lim
Production Manager: Chuck Harper

ATTENTION: SCHOOLS AND BUSINESSES
Andrews McMeel books are available at quantity discounts with bulk purchase for educational, business, or sales promotional use. For information, please e-mail the Andrews McMeel Publishing Special Sales Department: specialsales@amuniversal.com.